JOHN MARSHALL

The man who made
the Court supreme

by BILL SEVERN

jacket by Rus Anderson

Best known as the Chief Justice whose historic decisions established the power and durability of the Supreme Court as an independent and equal branch of government, and who gave the bare bones of the Constitution flesh and blood, John Marshall is less known for the human qualities that made him a warm-hearted and fun-loving man whose entire life was a romantic adventure.

With the accent on the man and the personal experiences that shaped his achievements, this inspiring biography shows how an unschooled backwoods boy with an uncommon genius for common sense learned from the time and place in which he lived a courage, directness and clear-mindedness that weighed more in his judgments than technical knowledge of law.

Born in the Virginia wilderness he hardly left until he was a young man, a virile son of the frontier, Marshall grew with the nation he loved and helped found. Here is the lively story of his adventures as a fighting minuteman, his courage as an officer in the

(continued on back flap)

JOHN MARSHALL

THE MAN WHO MADE
THE COURT SUPREME

By BILL SEVERN

DAVID McKAY COMPANY, INC.   NEW YORK

JOHN MARSHALL:
The Man Who Made the Court Supreme

LIBRARY OF CONGRESS CATALOG CARD NUMBER: 69-13784

MANUFACTURED IN THE UNITED STATES OF AMERICA

Typography by Charles M. Todd

JOHN MARSHALL

The Man Who Made the Court Supreme

JOHN MARSHALL was fourteen before he went to school. He stayed about a year and that was all the classroom schooling he had as a boy. But he had been reading books almost since he first learned to walk. With his father for a teacher, he was far better educated than most grown men of those days, many of whom could neither read nor write their own names. And he was growing up in a time and place that shaped him more than all his other learning.

Born in the Virginia wilderness, he hardly left until he was a young man. A virile son of the frontier, he grew with the nation he loved and helped found. Its history was made of events he lived through, and they also made him the man he became. His historic decisions that would establish the power and durability of the Supreme Court as an equal and independent branch of government, and that would give the bare bones of the Constitution flesh and blood, rested more upon the experiences of his life than on what he learned of law.

He didn't know at fourteen that he wanted to be Chief Justice of the United States, because there was no United States. But he did know he wanted to be a lawyer, and perhaps someday a member of Virginia's colonial House of

Burgesses as his father was. So his father agreed to send him off for a year's intensive study at the best school in the colony, the Reverend Archibald Campbell's Classical Academy in Westmoreland County.

It was a journey of one hundred miles from home, days and nights of travel over forest trails and primitive roads. John had never been away from home, but he had practically lived in the woods and he had no fear of making the long trip alone into the Potomac tidewater country. Yet it was like another world to him, with its rich plantations, its manor houses patterned after those of England, and the wealthy and aristocratic people, dressed in such finery as he had only imagined.

That was the part of Virginia where his father had been born, but Thomas Marshall had been neither rich nor the owner of more than a poor scrap of worn out tobacco land. Grandson of a carpenter and son of a small planter, Thomas was descended from plain people who first came from England around 1650. He did have ambition that pushed him from one frontier to another, always increasing his lands and profiting from them, and he taught himself to read and write and picked up a working knowledge of surveying, a trade much in demand among land-hungry Virginians.

Among the gentry of Westmoreland County were the Washingtons, and Thomas Marshall was George Washington's boyhood friend. The Washington family was connected by marriage with Lord Fairfax, holder of hundreds of thousands of acres of a huge colonial estate granted by the Kings of England. Under Lord Fairfax's gentlemanly influences, Thomas was a frequent borrower of books from the Fairfax library, and learned to appreciate a way of life different from his own.

When Lord Fairfax chose young Washington to help survey the Northern Neck lands across the Blue Ridge Mountains, George took his pal Thomas along as his assistant. The two teen-agers spent most of the next three years together, sharing crude shelters or sleeping in the woods, tracking through unexplored forests to mark out frontier boundaries. It was an experience that gave Thomas not only a restless and never-satisfied desire to seek new places, but also the knowledge that let him acquire promising lands of his own.

Thomas Marshall was twenty-four when he settled for a time in what was then Prince William and later Fauquier County, near a colony of Germans who worked nearby iron mines. There he met and married seventeen-year-old Mary Randolph Keith, daughter of the area's elderly Episcopal clergyman, sweeping her off her feet and away from her many other suitors. Pretty and vivacious, she was also high-born, a descendant of one of Virginia's great families, the Randolphs of Turkey Island, and a cousin of Jeffersons and Lees.

Thomas promptly carried his bride away to a little log cabin high on the mountain slope at the very edge of the forest, where he cleared land for planting, acted as a surveyor, and was a part-time agent for Lord Fairfax. John Marshall was born there on September 24, 1755, the first of their fifteen children.

Two brothers and two sisters soon made it a busy as well as a crowded cabin, but as busy as John's mother was she began to teach him his first reading lessons while he was still small enough to be held on her lap. Frontier living forced her to pin her clothes with thorns from bushes in place of buttons, but books the Marshalls had, even if only a few. As an unusually well-educated woman, she saw to it that distance from civilization didn't deprive her first-born son of learning.

From his father, John learned to love the outdoors, to walk quietly through the stillness of the woods with the spring of pine needles beneath his feet, to explore the dew-fresh fields of morning, and in the evening to sit and watch in wonder as sunset came. He learned to fish and to hunt, not just for sport but for needed family food, and to climb trees, pitch horseshoes, ride a horse.

There were no toys to play with, no ready-made amusements, but he had birds and small animals for pets, and when he wasn't busy doing chores he made his own fun with the pocket treasures of a few polished stones or bits of homespun yarn. All the family clothing was homespun and home-sewn. Food was plentiful, but simple and not varied. Years later he still remembered what a special mealtime treat it was to have cornmeal mush flavored with the balm of bay leaves.

When John was about nine, the Marshalls moved still deeper into the wilderness but not to another log cabin. Thomas Marshall had become somewhat a man of means and importance. Chosen sheriff of newly formed Fauquier County, he was about to become county clerk, head of the church vestry, and to be elected by his backwoods neighbors to the House of Burgesses.

On a 350-acre estate at Goose Creek, some twenty miles over the Blue Ridge Mountains from the nearest large settlement at Warrenton, he built the family a two-story frame house, with large rooms and a big stone fireplace downstairs and loftlike bedrooms above. Set high in the valley against the purple hills, it overlooked a broad stretch of sloping fields and a swift-running stream. Called "The Hollow," it became the home of John's years of growing to young manhood.

By then his father was carefully guiding his reading. "He superintended my education," John later wrote, "and gave me my early taste for history and poetry, and to his care I am indebted for anything valuable I learned in my youth."

John read the Bible, of course, from which he could quote chapter and verse. From Shakespeare, he learned the power of drama and the imagery of words, and a lifelong love of theater although he had never yet seen a stage. But it was from the English poets—Milton, Dryden, and especially

Alexander Pope—that his mind took the most. Before he was twelve he had copied out by hand nearly all of poet-moralist Pope's lengthy *Essay on Man,* as an exercise in the precise use of language and literary style.

Poetry forever inspired him, became his consolation and delight. He always preferred reading poetry and fiction to heavier tomes of law, and writing it became a means of expressing both his sense of humor and his deepest personal feelings. As a boy he recited it aloud, standing alone in clearings in the woods, where he also acted out parts of plays or delivered orations from the history books he read, imagining himself some dramatic or romantic character as he spoke to no audience but the trees.

But for all the wilderness isolation of his home, he was far from lonely. Another sister, two more brothers, and then again a sister were born at The Hollow, each a year apart. As the oldest, it was John's task to help manage the spirited brood. He took them out to play, comforted them, answered their questions, settled their quarrels, taught them their games, and there were always one or two happily tagging along with him as he performed his chores.

Although it meant long walks through the woods to join them, there were neighboring youths his own age for the sports of swimming, running races, and pitching horseshoes. But they were no companions for his mind. Few of them had ever seen a book, let alone try to read one, and as he later put it the time spent with them was entirely in "hardy exercise." His father was "my only intelligent companion" and "both a watchful parent and an affectionate and instructive friend."

On surveying trips as his father's helper, he learned to apply mathematics, measuring off the land with rod and chain. Their travels together through the woods were a time for serious talks about the growing oppression of British colonial rule, the increasing rebellion of Virginians who were demanding

the people's right to govern themselves. Resting under the
trees out of the hot sun, he and his father also talked of his
ambition to become a lawyer, and it was out of those talks
that the decision came to send him to the Academy in far-off
Westmoreland County, to give him the advantage of classroom
schooling very few boys had.

The Reverend Campbell's Academy was small enough to
allow individual instruction, and Campbell was a sound classical scholar, a learned graduate of Scotland's best universities,
whose reputation attracted pupils from the rich plantation
homes. There, at fourteen, John got not only a grounding in
Latin, history, philosophy, and ancient literature, but a view
of social graces and refinements lacking in his frontier home.
Among his closest schoolmate friends was James Monroe, a
gangling lad three years his junior.

Brought home after a year at the Academy, he was tutored
by another Scotch clergyman, the Reverend James Thompson.
He was the new minister at the church whose vestry Thomas
Marshall headed and he lived at the Marshall home. Sharing a
bedroom loft with John, he also became his counselor, guide,
and friend. Along with teaching the lyric Latin poetry of
Horace and Livy's vivid *History of Rome,* he quickened John's
mind to the closer events that were shaping history in Virginia.
A fiery young clergyman, later accused of treason against the
Crown for preaching thunderous sermons denouncing British
misrule, Thompson was a zealous champion of colonial
freedom.

But John's father was the better teacher of those events. In
the House of Burgesses, Thomas Marshall had become a
leader of the buckskin-shirted mountain men who fought the
controlling aristocracy that gained its affluence from British
trade. John heard first-hand from him the drama and conflict
of the great debates in which he stood firmly with his friends

George Washington and Patrick Henry against the edicts of the King.

Listening to his father vividly describe his own part in the historic protest against the Stamp Act, it was as if he had been there himself. In his mind, John could hear the Tory cries of "Treason, treason!" that interrupted Patrick Henry, and Henry's ringing reply, "If *this* be treason, make the most of it!"

When John was eighteen, the Marshalls moved a little nearer to Warrenton, to a place at the western foot of Cobbler's Mountain. His father had become one of the landed gentry and the estate spread out over several thousand acres. The seven-room house he built and called Oak Hill was the most elegant for miles around, with the first glass windows in that part of Virginia.

John had begun his self-study of law and every few weeks he hiked eighteen miles over the mountains to borrow books from an attorney's office in Warrenton, so he could read them at night by the fireside. But his deepest study was of the books his father bought for his benefit, *Blackstone's Commentaries*. Already famous in England for their simplicity, completeness and uniform logic, and for the poetic charm of their literary style, they were to become the backbone of early American law. Thomas Marshall was one of the original subscribers to the first-published American edition, and John steeped himself in Blackstone, but not for long.

The "controversy between Great Britain and her colonies had assumed so serious an aspect as almost to monopolize attention," he explained years afterwards, and he "engaged in it with all the zeal and enthusiasm which belonged to my age." Blackstone was put aside as he "devoted more time to learning the rudiments of military exercise."

Ever since news had reached Virginia of the Boston Tea Party, revolution had seemed almost sure to come. As a trained officer of the militia that first had been raised for protection against the Indians, Thomas Marshall felt it was his duty to instruct his sons. So John and his brothers and some of his friends had been parading up and down with their hunting muskets, drilling in the manual of arms.

Then word came from New England of the first open shots exchanged between British soldiers and the patriots of Lexington and Concord. In Virginia, Thomas Marshall went off to Richmond as a delegate to the Virginia Convention, to support the resolutions for the arming and defense of the colony. He came back to Oak Hill, gathered the family at the fireside, and solemnly told them the call had been given and there would be war. Once again, in his father's voice, John heard Patrick Henry speak:

"Is life so dear or peace so sweet to be purchased at the price of chains and slavery? Forbid it, Almighty God.... I know not what course others may take, but as for me, give me liberty or give me death."

With Thomas Marshall as its major and John helping to organize it, Fauquier and two neighboring counties raised Virginia's first regiment of minutemen. On the day in May, 1775, when John's company mustered, the captain who was expected to take command failed to show up, so John was named lieutenant and put in charge. Just out of his teens, he had no experience in leading men, but he put them through their first drill and then circled them around him and said that if they "wished to hear more about the war" he would tell them "what I understand about it."

Six feet tall, straight, slender, but with "a body that indicated agility rather than strength," according to one of the men who was there, he was "of dark complexion ... eyes dark to blackness, strong and penetrating ... hair raven black." Wearing a homespun "purple or pale blue hunting shirt and trousers of the same material, fringed with white" and a "round black hat, mounted with the buck's tail for a cockade," he "addressed the company for something like an hour."

He told them the time had come "to brighten our firearms and learn to use them in the field" and spoke of freedom and independence and of their rights that were at stake. Then he put his company at ease and turned the rest of the day to fun, joining them in foot races and other sports.

The drills went on through the summer and the men took to wearing uniforms of a sort, each with a bucktailed hat like his and a shirt on which mother or sister had sewn the white letters: "Liberty or Death!" But their pants were those they used for hunting, any bright color that happened to be spun at home, and in their belts they carried hunting knives and tomahawks.

Finally the citizen soldiers of revolution who had been "raised in a minute and armed in a minute" also marched in a minute. An express rider from Williamsburg brought news that the Royal Governor, Lord Dunmore, had proclaimed martial law and was arming additional men and stockpiling weapons. The minutemen were commanded to action. John Marshall's company ended their patriotic parading and marched off to help overthrow the government of the King's Colony of Virginia.

THEY WERE a wild looking bunch of radicals, that fierce rebel band of rag-tag mountain men who came down out of the woods with John Marshall seven months before the Declaration of Independence to march across Virginia to the sea. Roughly dressed, long hair hanging loose, brandishing knives and shouldering muskets, they waved the rattlesnake flag of revolution with its defiant warning: "Don't tread on me!"

In the eyes of loyal British colonists, they were an uncivilized mob, a rabble that had risen from the hills to destroy established law and order. Their savage appearance terrified much of the countryside. Respectable people, wrote one chronicler of the march, seemed "as much afraid of us as if we were Indians."

Doors of homes were barred against them in fear. But if the aristocrats were alarmed, the common people generally sympathized with their cause. Marshall's frontiersmen "took pride in demeaning ourselves as patriots and gentlemen" and most people soon relaxed and treated them "with respect and great kindness."

British sympathizers spread hysterical warnings ahead of

them to Governor Dunmore and he cautioned his royal troops that a fight to the death would be better than captivity because if they fell into the hands of the "shirt men," they would be tortured and scalped. But by the time Marshall's men and other companies had reached the colonial capital at Williamsburg, Lord Dunmore had fled aboard a man-of-war to Norfolk.

Under martial law, he had proclaimed as traitors all men who did not rally to His Majesty's cause and take a stern oath of allegiance to support his regular troops, and he also had promised freedom to Negro slaves who deserted their rebel owners to help build fortifications. Governor Dunmore made his stand at the Great Bridge, twelve miles from Norfolk on the only good road.

On land surrounded by swamp, where his cannon could command the bridge and its approach, he built a well-protected fort. The minutemen drew up opposite it and threw a defensive breastwork across the causeway, but while they outnumbered the British they had no cannon and dared not attack. For several days in early December, 1775, both sides held their positions.

Legend has it that a patriotic Negro slave, posing as a runaway and a deserter to the British, was sent to Lord Dunmore by the minutemen as a secret agent who broke the stalemate and lured the British out of their fort to defeat. Under questioning, according to the story, he deliberately gave false information that convinced the British that the rebels were only a small force of poorly armed men.

Dunmore ordered his troops to attack and at daybreak on December 9, Captain Fordyce led his Royal Grenadiers out of their protective fort and marched them six-abreast into the fire of the waiting Americans. The British captain "fell dead within a few steps of the breastwork," Marshall later wrote, and "every Grenadier was killed or wounded; while the Americans did not lose a single man."

The British abandoned their fort, spiked their cannon and fled, with the minutemen in pursuit. Dunmore and the remainder of his troops boarded ships waiting in the harbor and Marshall's company and the others took over Norfolk. Marshall was there at the start of the new year, 1776, when Dunmore had his men-of-war cannonade Norfolk from the harbor. British sailors came ashore, set waterfront tobacco warehouses on fire, and started a conflagration that raged three days and destroyed the town.

Virginia's war was halted for a time and Marshall's military services were not needed by the state. Discharged, he went home to Fauquier County, where he might have sat out the bigger war as many Americans did. But he didn't stay long in the mountains at Oak Hill. Instead of a temporary militiaman, he became an officer in the nation's army.

George Washington had been named Commander in Chief by the Continental Congress in Philadelphia. Marshall's cousin, Thomas Jefferson, was writing the Declaration of Independence before returning to Virgina as its wartime governor. Marshall traded the hunting shirt, fringed leggings and bucktailed hat of the minutemen for the buff and blue uniform and tricorn hat of the Continental Army. Commissioned a lieutenant of the Third Virginia Regiment, of which his father was major, he went off to join Washington's troops.

By the time he reached New Jersey in the late summer of 1776, Washington's army was in retreat. He came to it with fresh enthusiasm, eager to press the war forward, but spent the next months fleeing from the British and fighting delaying skirmishes. Driven out of New York, weary, footsore and despondent, it was an army poorly equipped, clothed and fed. Held together less by any unifying government authority than by devotion of its men to Washington as commander, it was a force in which each separate state put its own interests first.

For Marshall, that was the start of a painful education in

the need for strong central government. The relationship between the states and the national government was to be the basic conflict of his life. His first lesson came from the wartime danger, misery and ordeals caused as much by a powerless Congress as by the enemy.

"I had grown up at a time ... when the maxim 'United we stand; divided we fall' was the maxim of every orthodox American," he was to write, "and I had imbued these sentiments so thoroughly that they constituted a part of my being. I carried them with me into the Army, where I found myself associated with brave men from different states, who were risking life and everything valuable in a common cause believed by all to be most precious, and where I was confirmed in the habit of considering America as my country and Congress as my government."

Some states sent the Army a full quota of men and others didn't. Units came and went as they pleased, serving a few weeks and then returning home, sometimes leaving on the eve of battle. Whole regiments dwindled away overnight. Entire companies were reduced to a few men. Commanders never knew how many troops they could count on.

Jealous of other states and fiercely independent of national command, each state militia fought what amounted to its own war in its own way, enforcing its own rules so that general discipline became almost impossible. Incompetent officers were appointed for political reasons. There was dishonesty and waste, supplies bought that were never delivered, men paid who never served. Some soldiers were supplied by their states with good weapons and others had nearly none. A soldier from one state was well-clothed and the next man in rags; some had shoes and others walked barefoot.

Marshall knew the bravery of the men beside him, their readiness to give even their lives for freedom. Matched against that, he saw the want of arms and of food, the disorder and unnecessary suffering. Day by day, the knowledge was forced upon him that the government had no practical unity, no true authority, that Congress was without power and could only pass along whatever the states were willing to dole out to it.

An army in retreat requires a different courage from its officers than an army of victory and Marshall proved himself well. He lifted the sinking spirits of his men with jokes and stories, kept them active with sports and games, turned their grumbling discontent to hard laughter. His reputation for calm good humor and understanding leadership spread beyond his own company, and it was that more than military prowess which won him promotion to captain-lieutenant and transfer to the Fifteenth Virginia Line.

When British General William Howe successfully invaded Pennsylvania, Marshall was chosen by General Washington as one of a specially picked band of nine officers and a hundred soldiers to harass the British advance while the main army moved into positions along Brandywine Creek. Without artillery and knowing they couldn't hold their stand for long, they met the enemy on the road at Iron Hill. In Marshall's first direct fighting since Norfolk, nearly half the Americans were killed or wounded before he and the survivors fell back under orders.

In the major battle of Brandywine that followed, with bitter defeat for the Americans, Marshall saw the fatal consequences of having troops supplied by individual states. "Many of their muskets were scarcely fit for service, and being of unequal caliber their cartridges could not be well-fitted," he wrote, "and this radical defect was felt in all the operations of the Army."

Through most of a bloody September day he fought the British at the left of the American line, while his father held an advanced position at the right. Colonel Thomas Marshall had his forces cut to pieces and two horses shot out from under him; Captain-lieutenant John Marshall showed his courage in skirmish after skirmish. But finally the British charged in a dense mass across the Brandywine, the lines crumbled and the Americans were routed. Nearly one thousand Americans were killed or wounded and four hundred taken prisoner.

Marshall marched his retreating men for a day and a night through cold rain to a place of safety. When he inspected their weapons he found flimsy gunlocks had come loose, muskets were so fouled they were no better than clubs, and because cartridge boxes were improperly made "scarcely one cartridge in a box was fit for use."

The Americans were in no condition to fight, but Congress angrily demanded that General Washington block the British march on the capital city of Philadelphia. For weeks, the Army maneuvered through mud and half-frozen streams, without enough men, weapons, tents, shoes, clothes or food. The British could not be stopped. They occupied Philadelphia, placing most of their forces at Germantown, and the impotent Congress fled to York.

When Washington tried a daring surprise attack on Germantown in October, Marshall again was in the thick of fighting. The British first gave ground but heavy fog and blundering poor judgment by American officers gave the enemy a chance to reorganize and to hold Philadelphia, and chase Washington's bedraggled Army into the hills. But the British failed to follow up their advantage and they let the Americans escape, to wait for weeks in the woods, daily expecting attack before they finally made their way to the winter camp that became the horror of Valley Forge.

In that winter of historic misery when nakedness, starvation and disease became more the enemies than the British, Marshall saw men huddled by twelves in log huts where the well barely had space to lie with the untended dying. He saw hundreds who for want of blankets had to sit up all night without sleep, afraid that to lie down would be to freeze. On Christmas Eve he watched men eat watery soup as their only meal. The day after Christmas his soldiers waded through snow to their knees, snow soon red from their bleeding naked feet.

He knew that neighboring farmers, with no concern for a nation or its Army, were smuggling beef and other food through to Philadelphia where the comfortable British Army would pay hard money for it, instead of the money of Congress that was "not worth a Continental." Even provisions bought and paid for were diverted by dishonesty and greed. Blankets, shirts, and shoes were stolen before they reached the Army. Marshall himself had only one shirt, so that when he washed it he had to wrap his bare shoulders in a rough rag of blanket.

Washington could beg Congress for help and Congress could plead with the states, but the states did as they pleased and often what they did was ignore Congress. Soldiers bitterly cursed the powerless government and many besides Marshall who lived through that winter had their political beliefs fixed for them by the need they knew for a government of authority as well as liberty.

By February less than one-third of the seventeen thousand soldiers camped at Valley Forge were fit for service. Four thousand were confined to their huts by plain nakedness, forced to stay indoors because they had nothing to cover them from the cold. Scores died of starvation and others were too feeble to stand. Marshall was one of the few who stayed healthy and perhaps that helped him keep his spirit.

Lieutenant Philip Slaughter, his messmate, remembered him as "the best-tempered man I ever knew." To Slaughter, Marshall was "an excellent companion, and idolized by the soldiers and his brother officers, whose gloomy hours were enlivened by his inexhaustible fund of anecdote." When other officers complained, "he would shame them by good-natured raillery, or encourage them by his own exuberance." Years afterwards, Slaughter recalled how Marshall turned one particular night of desperation to laughter by donning a pair of tattered silk stockings and acting the clown.

Appointed a Deputy Judge Advocate of the Army, Marshall decided disputes between officers and men, settled quarrels, and ruled on cases involving violation of military regulations. Some were petty and some serious, but they called less for legal knowledge than good judgment. He gained a reputation for weighing both sides of even minor questions and for making written instead of spoken decisions, so every man clearly understood his reasoning. It was a position that brought him into closer personal association with Washington as well as with Colonel Alexander Hamilton and other high officers, and on a lower level of rank he made many Army friends who later were important to his career.

When spring came and the shad began to run in the Schuylkill River there was food at last for the hungry men. The fish helped save what was left of Washington's Army, and the men came out of their smoky, disease-ridden huts of winter into the sun. Slowly they regained their strength for drills and body-building exercise. Marshall led the outdoor sports. "He could throw a quoit farther, and beat at a race any other," one of the soldiers noted, and he was the only one among the officers who "with a running jump, could clear a stick laid on the heads of two men as tall as himself." His mother had sent him some socks with heels made of white yarn and Marshall showed those heels to so many he beat at foot races that he was nicknamed "Silver Heels."

In May, 1778, inspiring word reached camp of the French alliance with America against Britain, and meanwhile there were intelligence reports from Philadelphia that Sir Henry Clinton, the new British commander, had decided to move out of that city and return his forces to New York by land. On June 18, Clinton set his troops in motion to abandon Philadelphia and General Washington put his revived Army in quick pursuit.

Ten days later the Americans caught up with the British near Monmouth, New Jersey. Washington's generals voted against going into immediate battle, but he overruled them. Marshall's division was given orders to attack the British columns as soon as they broke camp. Struggling through mud and sand on the hottest day of the year, they suffered nearly as much from thirst and swarms of Jersey mosquitoes as from the British. Night fell with no decision, but when the men awoke at dawn to fight again, the British were gone.

The Americans had won a victory, but the British moved on toward New York. Congress returned to the capital at Philadelphia and Marshall was made a full captain as he marched along with Washington's Army in pursuit of the British.

The war dragged into another year for him. In July, 1779, he took part in the assault on Stony Point, then spent weeks with a small scouting party dangerously probing the edge of the British line. In August he was one of the raiders who swept deep inside enemy territory at Paulus Hook.

But by the end of 1779 enlistments had begun expiring in the Virginia regiments. The ranks were so thinned there were more officers than men to command. Captain Marshall was ordered to return to Virginia to await the hoped for action of the legislature in raising new troops. On December 9, while Washington's command began settling into another winter's quarters at Morristown, Marshall set out for home.

The letters he had been writing home, like those of most men at war, had been read aloud to friends, and among those who heard them was a fourteen-year-old girl in Yorktown, where Marshall's father had been stationed. From all she heard about him, she had begun to fall in love with him before she ever saw him. As soon as he saw her, he fell in love, too, and loved her devotedly and romantically the rest of his life.

3

MARY AMBLER, called "Polly," was the daughter of a man who had been among Yorktown's wealthiest, until the war ruined him financially. But Jacquelin Ambler still was a powerful man in Virginia, a Councillor of State who served among the leaders of resistance to the British in the nearby capital at Williamsburg. His home in Yorktown was next to the military headquarters commanded by Colonel Thomas Marshall.

Colonel Marshall was the Amblers' good friend and he naturally talked a lot about his son, read his letters to them, made Polly and her sisters feel they knew John well. As a dashing young officer of the Revolution, John became something of a dream hero to the girls. "Every line received from him was heard with rapture," according to Polly's older sister Eliza, until they thought of him as "a very paragon."

When the Ambler girls learned he was coming for a reunion with his father shortly before Christmas in 1779, they spread the word among their friends and all the daughters of Yorktown's patriots soon were "on tiptoe" with excitement, Eliza noted, their romantic expectations "raised to the highest pitch."

Yorktown's young society centered around the Ambler girls, not only because of their father's influence in Virginia affairs of state, but because they apparently were the most attractive girls for miles around. Their mother had been a celebrated beauty, Rebecca Burwell, the lost love of Thomas Jefferson's youth. She was the "Belinda" to whom Jefferson wrote infatuated and impassioned love letters. Now Jefferson was Virginia's governor and she was Jacquelin Ambler's wife, and the four Ambler girls seemingly had inherited much of her beauty and charm. When they decided to plan a ball to welcome Captain Marshall, their friends excitedly fell in with their plan and soon were gossiping over the details of "who should first be introduced."

Polly, just fourteen, was the quiet one of the family, a pale, repressed, nervously timid girl, with what her sister Eliza called "a delicacy of frame and feeling that baffles all description." Polly astonished her more socially active friends by telling them that, as Eliza wrote, "she, for the first time, had made up her mind to go to the ball, though she had not even been at dancing school." Polly informed them that they were giving themselves "useless trouble" arguing over who would have the first dance with Captain Marshall because she "was resolved to set her cap at him and eclipse us all."

But John Marshall turned out to be a distinct disappointment to most of the girls when he showed up for the ball. They had been "expecting an Adonis," as Eliza put it, a handsome, smartly dressed young captain who would sweep them off their feet with his courtly flattery and polished social graces. Instead, he was a tall, gaunt, slovenly dressed and war-weary soldier, awkward and ill at ease in the ballroom. "I, for one, lost all desire of becoming agreeable in his eyes," Eliza admitted, "when I beheld his awkward figure, unpolished manners and total neglect of person."

Polly wasn't disappointed, and John was "greatly pleased

with her." From the moment of their introduction, as he later wrote, they "formed a strong attachment." It soon was strong enough that he "would have climbed Alleghenies of skulls and swum Atlantics of blood to have her." He was, in Eliza's words, "an enthusiast in love," and he wooed Polly as ardently as he had fought as a soldier.

Whatever he lacked in appearance, he seemed to make up for in personality. He became popular with nearly everybody in Yorktown, but the Ambler home was the one he visited most. In the evenings, by parlor candlelight, he read poetry aloud by the hour to Polly. Even Eliza had somewhat sisterly second thoughts and noted that "our whole family became attached to him" and "from the moment he loved my sister he became truly a brother to me."

Still without an Army assignment, and with new reason to think about the future, he decided to make use of his time and also stay close to Polly by entering William and Mary College at Williamsburg, a dozen miles away. A course of lectures in "Law and Police," the first college law course to be given in America, was starting its first classes under Professor George Wythe, whose teachings were to influence a whole generation of outstanding men. Tuition was one thousand pounds of tobacco, which Thomas Marshall was able to provide for his son, though like almost everybody else in Virginia he was hard-pressed for ready cash.

John Marshall's political and social connections, and the fact that he was older than most of his classmates and a returned veteran and officer, undoubtedly helped him become a class leader at little William and Mary. Within two weeks, he was captaining the debating team and was made a member of the parent chapter of just-formed Phi Beta Kappa fraternity, which was to become the academic honor society. But his personality also counted. He was a leader as well of fun and

pranks, including some finger-scribbling in the wet plaster of
a college hall.

It was a democratic campus, even though expense restricted
college education to the well-to-do and the students were
mostly sons of distinguished Virginia families. They shared
meals along with the five professors at a common dining table,
and were allowed to go without coats or shoes in warm
weather. There was a fine library, from which John borrowed
many books he carried off to Yorktown for his poetry readings to Polly. He enjoyed the shared evenings of song, drink
and talk with classmates, but the attractions of Yorktown were
stronger and kept his horse busy carrying him those twelve
familiar miles.

Professor Wythe's course was intensive, ranging over the
whole body of law, and Marshall filled dozens of pages of a
thick leather-bound book with notes, each page headed by the
topic of the lectures, which spanned subjects from Annuity,
and Assault and Battery, to Elections, Leases and Legacies.
There were also regular sessions of a mock court, at which
Wythe and other professors sat as judges while Marshall and
his fellow students conducted assigned cases before a public
audience of "the most respectable Citizens." To instruct them
in parliamentary rules, Wythe formed a student legislature and
had them draw up original bills and debate, amend and revise
laws.

But though he studied hard. Marshall's mind wandered
from the lectures to Polly, and he doodled her name and his
thoughts about her all over the pages of his notebook. The
evidence of what was really on his mind was found in those
notes years later, sometimes scrawled, sometimes printed,
even written upside down on the corners of pages: "Miss
M. Ambler. . . . Miss Polly Am. . . . John Marshall, Miss
Maria. . . ."

He was stunned when he received news that Polly would

be moving away, not a world away but beyond courting distance. Her father had been made state treasurer and in the face of threatened British occupation of Williamsburg, Governor Jefferson had ordered the state capital removed to the little trading town of Richmond. Polly would have to go with the family.

The Amblers moved in late June, but on their way spent a few days in Williamsburg and Marshall and his friends organized a ball to honor the Ambler girls. He danced with Polly and afterwards walked her home along the starlit street, and at their wistful parting made the sudden resolve to quit college and follow her to Richmond. He had hardly more than begun his studies at William and Mary, but he was a man who had gone through war, and was in love and wanted to marry.

Abruptly, in the midst of his first term, he left college and never returned. Those five weeks were all the formal law education he ever had. He had gained some grounding in the spirit and tradition of law, had read Blackstone and would continue law readings. There really was no American law, since as yet there was no real American nation, and a lawyer's success depended less on knowing precedent than on experience, clear reasoning and common sense. But Marshall probably weighed none of those considerations; the decision was from his heart.

On a new page in his notebook, he wrote: "Polly Ambler, Richmond." He arrived there to find her father busy with state business and "acted Pa for a fortnight," helping the Amblers get settled in a rented cottage so small the whole family could "scarcely stand up altogether in it." Richmond, a farm trading center with tobacco warehouses its main business, had its small scatter of cottages "from the river to the hill" overcrowded by the sudden influx of state officials.

He took enough time out from courting Polly to ride over to one of the flimsy cabins erected as temporary state offices and apply for a license to practice law. His cousin, Thomas

Jefferson, signed it. Though they were cousins, they had been far apart for years, and were even further apart in their ideas.

Marshall had been learning in war the lessons of a new nationalism; Jefferson, already famous as the apostle of the rights of man, was opposed to a supreme centralized government and had left the Continental Congress in the hope of translating the people's revolution into the reality of Virginia's new state government. If Jefferson had guessed that day what his twenty-five-year-old cousin would make of the doctrine of Federal supremacy, he might have hesitated longer before giving him his license.

But Marshall took it and made a quick trip home to Fauquier County to take the necessary oaths there to be admitted to the bar on August 28, 1780. Before he could make any use of it, the British launched their invasion of Virginia and most of the state's courts were closed. Some of Marshall's feelings against the inefficiency of state governments, and particularly against Jefferson for failing to prepare stronger defense, grew out of the British invasion, headed by traitor Benedict Arnold.

As Captain John Marshall, he took to the battlefield again. With a small force of militiamen, he attempted to ambush a British landing party near the James River, not far from Richmond. But the Americans were outnumbered by the British and driven off. The British soon landed in strong force.

"What a panic for us all," Eliza wrote. "Governor, Council, everybody scampering. . . ." The terrified Amblers fled from Richmond to Hanover County, where they sought refuge in the country home of Polly's young cousin John Ambler, who was about to inherit one of Virginia's greatest fortunes. Soon they were fleeing again, from cabin to cabin, as Polly went through sleepless nights of fear.

Benedict Arnold led the invaders into Richmond and on January 5, 1781, pillaged the town before withdrawing. More

British landed and the whole countryside was harassed through the early months of spring. Frightened Virginians couldn't guess that decisive American and French military actions were to end the war with surrender at Yorktown before the year was over.

Captain Marshall still waited for Jefferson to raise new troops for him to command. He had no soldiers to lead and no courts in which to be a lawyer. So, as a man who soon hoped to marry and would have a family depending upon him, he decided to use the time to insure his future health by being inoculated against smallpox. He had been reading about it and had become convinced everyone should take that precaution. Because the laws of Virginia were against the new treatment, he walked all the way to Philadelphia. He made it on foot over the trails of four states at a speed of thirty-five miles a day.

He looked so disreputable when he reached Philadelphia, unshaved, hair matted and clothing stained, that he had a hard time convincing a tavern keeper to take him in for the night. Finally he got lodgings and the next day found a doctor who would perform the then daring inoculation. Feeling secure against the scourge, he hiked back to Virginia and Polly.

By then the Amblers had returned to Richmond and he discovered there was a rival for Polly's love, a Major Richard Anderson. Years afterwards he recalled his jealousy then as "our little tiffs and makings up." But at the time it apparently worried him enough so that he resigned his commission as an Army officer to get about the business of establishing a law practice so he could make Polly his wife.

He found little call for his law services. For months he anxiously traveled back and forth between Fauquier County, where he hoped his father's political prominence would get him clients, and Richmond, where Polly was. "All the thousand indescribable but deeply affecting instances of your affection or coldness," he told her later, "constituted for a time the happiness or misery of my life."

But Richmond, where his heart was, also was the center of the state's legal profession, and he finally resolved to quit chasing off into the mountains after clients and stay in Richmond by getting himself elected to Virginia's House of Delegates. With his father's support and his own popularity, especially among war veterans, Marshall was chosen a delegate from Fauquier County in the fall of 1782. As a member of the legislature, he would serve in Richmond, and his election to public office also would help him start there as a lawyer.

Family tradition had it that Marshall proposed and Polly hesitated, but when he rode off in farewell she burst into hysterics and sent word for him to return. Anyhow, she agreed to marry him and the date was set. Because the Ambler house in Richmond was too small for an elaborate ceremony, Polly's wealthy cousin, John Ambler, offered his country home in Hanover County for the wedding.

There at dusk on January 3, 1783, in high style in a candle-lit parlor filled with Marshalls and Amblers and a goodly gathering of Virginia aristocrats, Captain John Marshall took Mary Ambler as his bride. He was twenty-seven and she not quite seventeen. They moved into a one-story frame house in the Ambler back yard in Richmond and, as he wrote, "the woman I adored . . . (became) the chief happiness of my life."

>>> CHAPTER <<<

4

JOHN MARSHALL earned almost no money as a lawyer his first year in Richmond. His account book listed only four legal fees for the whole year and he spent more than that in a month on Polly and himself and the needs of their new household. But they faced no grinding hardships. There was income from some of the best farm land in Fauquier County, which his father had transferred to him, a small salary as a member of the legislature, and his credit was good. In the aftermath of war almost everybody lived on barter and promises.

His father, with a number of other children to bring up, was preparing to lead most of the family into the new frontier lands of the part of Virginia called Kentucky and settle there with them for the rest of his life. His friend, Daniel Boone, would guide them and Thomas Marshall soon would become one of Kentucky's leading citizens, as well as a delegate from there to the same Virginia legislature John Marshall served.

Before leaving for Kentucky, Thomas Marshall used his twenty-year accumulation of political friendships to better his son's standing in state government. State Treasurer Jacquelin Ambler, anxious to promote the success of his son-in-law, also did what he could, and Ambler was a man who could obtain any reasonable political favors he wanted. With their help and with his own ability, John Marshall quickly rose to legislative leadership.

Richmond was a crude little town of raw dirt streets, one church, one tavern, and no stone buildings, but it was growing fast and Virginia, as the country's first-ranking state in population, drew to its seat of government men who were to make it "the Athens of America." In its courts, Marshall would match his talent against outstanding lawyers, and in its legislature against those who were to be giants of the nation.

When he first took his seat, the House of Delegates met in a small barnlike structure used on other occasions as a community hall for dances, banquets and social affairs. But Thomas Jefferson was there, having returned to the legislature after being governor, and such other notable men as Patrick Henry, Richard Henry Lee, and later James Madison, George Mason and Edmund Randolph. Also serving with Marshall was his old schoolmate James Monroe, whose own political star was rising.

Marshall showed a willingness to work at the business of government and his early lack of law clients gave him plenty of time to devote to it. Most of the work was "done by a very few men," according to a visitor, and the rest "with little education or knowledge" merely "gave their votes." Legislators wandered in and out as they pleased, talked, laughed, told jokes, discussed horse races, and "were not quiet five minutes at a time."

Some could barely read or write. Living in distant parts of the state where there was little communication and where news was printed weeks late if at all, their information about issues before them was based mostly on rumor. Many attended sessions only when some bill vital to local interests came up and had no interest in measures that might affect others. For the most part, along with most Americans who had just thrown off British rule, they believed the least government was the best government. Educated men in fashionable attire mingled with woodsmen in fringed leggings and hunting shirts and with high-booted farmers in homespun clothing who chewed tobacco, spat as they pleased, and lounged with their feet on their desks.

Few were more carelessly dressed than Marshall, in a loosely comfortable shirt, short round-about jacket and rough trousers. Then as ever, he cared nothing about appearance, and was as informal in manner. Ready to shake any man's hand or clap a friendly arm around his shoulder, he was a big laughter-filled man who fitted well into that free-and-easy assembly. But on the more serious side, he had a swiftly recognized ability that won him more than his share of appointments to important committees to rewrite state laws for courts and elections, plan defenses, organize investigations, and reorganize the militia.

With the added powerful political influence of the Marshall and Ambler families behind him, after only eleven working days as a member of the House of Delegates, he was boosted into the highest position the legislature could offer. By a joint ballot of both houses, Marshall was elected to the Council of State, the executive council of eight men chosen from all of Virginia to serve as the governor's official cabinet. The governor was required by law to consult the Council on all important matters of state and to obtain its approval in appointing justices of peace, surveyors, tobacco inspectors and many state officers.

It was a boost that was too swift and too high to please some of Virginia's elder statesmen and it aroused resentful protest. The Council was supposed to be made up of men ripe in years who could guide the governor with advice based on long experience. Edmund Pendleton, Judge of the High Court of Chancery and President of the Court of Appeals, led the attack. "Young Mr. Marshall . . . is clever, but I think too young for that department," he wrote, saying a place on the Council should be earned as reward for "ten or twelve years hard service in the Assembly."

Other judges and prominent Virginians took up the criticism, but for a while Marshall rode out the storm. He was proud of his new position and was thoroughly enjoying his life in Richmond. His pretty bride had brought him into the full circle of society. They entertained frequently at home and were a shining young couple attending dances, dinners and horse races at the new track, or visiting the playhouse that had been set up by a company of actors in a large shed near the market.

His friend Monroe was a close companion of other activities. Both lost rather heavily at times playing cards and betting on the races, and together they enjoyed the boisterous male fellowship of the tavern, clubs and fraternal societies. When Monroe was elected to the Continental Congress and went off to Annapolis, where he shared a room with also-elected Thomas Jefferson and began to come under his political spell, Marshall kept him well-informed of the latest gossip in Richmond.

"The excessive cold weather has operated like magic on our youth," he wrote in one letter to Monroe. "They feel the necessity of artificial heat and quite wearied with lying alone all are treading the broad road to matrimony." Tabby Eppes, he reported, "has grown quite fat and buxom," and he named another girl who was "in high spirits over the success of her antique sister and firmly thinks her time will come next."

He also acted as his friend's lawyer in trying to collect money that the state owed Monroe while he held off the demands of those to whom Monroe owed money. Marshall's law practice had grown considerably, and so had the size of his fees. At the start, an average case brought him seven dollars, but within a year his average fee was twenty dollars and he sometimes got as much as seventy-five. His dealings as a lawyer were increasingly with men of capital and he was busy not only in Richmond but in the courts of Fauquier County and other parts of the state.

But he found his law practice coming into conflict with his position on the Council of State. Judge Pendleton and others had kept up their criticism. Some judges questioned whether it was proper for him to be appearing in courts as a lawyer at the same time he was advising the governor about the appointment of justices of the peace. Marshall finally decided he couldn't risk increasing the resentment of the judges in whose courts he had to argue cases and he resigned from the State Council.

However, he kept his seat in the House of Delegates, and Fauquier County sent him back for a second term. He no longer lived there, and Richmond was in Henrico County, but he owned the Marshall lands in Fauquier. That made him eligible and his former neighbors and father's friends still wanted him to represent them.

The hottest issue before the legislature was a boiling controversy over the peace treaty with Great Britain. Before the war Virginia's farmers and planters had ordered whatever they wanted from England, promising to pay for it with tobacco and other crops. English merchants extended easy credit, planters renewed their notes, and a mountain of debts piled up. Payments were halted by law during the war, since the British were the enemy, and when it ended the Virginians found themselves owing London mercantile houses between ten and fifteen million dollars, and had no ready cash to meet demands for payment. Virginia began passing a maze of laws to block collection of the debts. But one of the conditions of the peace treaty between Britain and the United States was that all laws that stood in the way of recovering the British debts would be removed.

Marshall felt it was a matter of national honor to meet the terms of the peace treaty. He believed that other nations of the world would look upon the new American government as no real government at all if individual states could ignore its treaties. Virginia's delaying tactics were, to him, an open breach of contract between the two countries and a violation of national faith. He sided with James Madison and others in upholding the treaty and demanding that Virginians pay their debts.

Two weeks after he took his seat in the legislature in 1784, he brought to a vote a resolution to repeal "every act or acts of the Assembly now in force in this Commonwealth as prevent due compliance with the stipulation contained in the definitive Treaty of Peace entered into between Great Britain and America."

It was defeated by twenty votes and the planters, with Patrick Henry championing their cause, proposed an alternate resolution that Virginia should not cooperate in carrying out the terms of the peace treaty until the British paid heavy war damages and surrendered some military outposts they still held in America. With passions inflamed, the battle went on through the whole session, and half a dozen attempts to repeal the anti-debt laws were defeated on one pretext or another.

Marshall wrote Monroe that the legislature was "tending to weaken the Federal bands, which in my conception are too weak already." Meanwhile he strongly opposed an act which postponed state tax payments and another designed to let Virginians pay up to half their taxes in commodities instead of money. He argued that no state with an empty treasury could have a strong government and that Virginia should not let its citizens get into the habit of regarding tax payments as less of an obligation than the payment of private debts.

His frustrations in the treaty and tax fights made him strongly critical of state government in general and the legislature in particular. He found his fellow legislators apathetic, avoiding firm decisions, and unwilling to pass laws that called upon the people to accept their responsibilities as citizens. Marshall complained in a letter to one friend that "this long session has not produced a single bill of public importance," and to another that the members seemed more interested in "private animosities" than in the public welfare. Their only desire, he thought, was to promote strictly local benefits, and they cared little about good state government or a strong nation.

The legislature finally did repeal the anti-debt laws so as to reluctantly give assent to the terms of the peace treaty with Britain, but Marshall was so disillusioned by then by what he considered its narrow view of state and national affairs that he decided not to seek re-election and took himself out of state politics for a year. "The general tendency of state politics convinced me," he later wrote, "that no safe and permanent remedy could be found but in a more efficient and better organized general (national) government."

His first son was born July 21, 1784, the first of ten children he and Polly would have in the next twenty years. Colonel Thomas Marshall had come from Kentucky for a visit and was on hand for the christening when the baby was named Thomas for him. As a well-settled family man, John Marshall cheerfully took on the responsibility of providing for other relatives. His seventeen-year-old sister Lucy came to live with him and Polly in Richmond, and their parlor became the place of her courting by Polly's wealthy cousin John Ambler, whom Lucy later married.

Marshall saw to it that Lucy had every advantage a young girl needed to launch her properly in Richmond society. He bought her clothes, had her tutored, sent her to dancing school, and Polly, who was only two years older, also took her sister-in-law socially under her wing. Marshall was as generous with financial support, help and advice to his younger brother James, who had remained in Virginia when the rest of the Marshalls went to Kentucky, and he was constantly doing things for all the Amblers, especially Polly's sister Eliza who called him "my darling brother Marshall."

Able to buy a new house for his family, on spacious tree-shaded grounds across from the home of Polly's parents, Marshall converted one of the frame outbuildings near the edge of the lot into a small office and began to buy law books for it. For his home library, he bought mostly novels and books of poetry and plays, but also many-volumed sets of lectures, biographies and history. Polly, he wrote, "had a fine taste for belle-lettre reading" which she "judiciously applied in the selection of pieces she admired."

But tragedy shadowed their happiness. Polly, never in robust health, was stricken with a disease of the nervous system from which she never fully recovered. Physicians of those years, with their limited knowledge, were baffled by it. Marshall called in three of Richmond's best doctors, but they were of little help. Family reticence kept him and others from revealing the details, but her sister Eliza wrote that Polly became "a prey to an extreme nervous affliction which more or less embittered her comfort through life."

The rest of their years together she was subject to nervous seizures that at times left her completely helpless. Marshall hired a housekeeper, bought Polly a horse to ride for exercise, and a carriage to take her on quiet rides in the country when she was afraid to go riding by herself. Sudden noises disturbed her so that he took to walking about the house in stocking feet, hushing the children, and even getting up in the middle of the night to chase animals away from outside, to keep dogs from barking or stray cows from bawling.

Still, she remained to Marshall "the wife, the mother, the mistress of a family, and the friend" and physically and mentally the "agreeable companion . . . of those winter evenings during which her protracted ill health and her feeble nervous system confined us entirely to each other." According to Eliza, her sister's troubles "only served to increase his care and tenderness," and after a long lifetime with hardly a day wherever he was that he failed to worry over Polly's well-being, he described her to an intimate friend as "a most devoted wife ... cheerful, mild, benevolent, serious, humane" and with "a judgment so sound and so safe that I have often relied upon it in situations of perplexity."

Polly appeared in public less often, but the Marshalls entertained almost as they always had at home. Monroe and Madison were among frequent guests, as were other important men. Patrick Henry, although by then Marshall's political opponent, came to their dinner parties, especially when his old friend Thomas Marshall was staying with his son in Richmond as a Kentucky delegate to the legislature.

Albert Gallatin, then a young Swiss interpreter who had come to Richmond to try to collect some of the pre-war debts Virginians owed a foreign banking house, was among those who enjoyed Marshall's "proverbial Virginia hospitality." They became such close friends Marshall tried to talk him into entering the legal profession and "offered to take me into his office without a fee and assured me I would become a distinguished lawyer." Gallatin instead later became Jefferson's political adviser, Secretary of the Treasury, and the genius who reshaped the nation's financial structure. "John Marshall, though but a young lawyer in 1783," Gallatin wrote, "was almost at the head of the bar in 1786."

Marshall's growing fame as an outstanding lawyer was becoming generally recognized. Richmond had even begun to take democratic pride in the fact that his disregard for his appearance more often made him look like a town tramp. What was comfortable was what he wore, and he seldom seemed aware of what he had on as long as it decently covered him and suited the weather. He simply refused to fuss over the conformities of fashion that others appeared to take so seriously.

Richmond hugely enjoyed a story that was being told in the taverns about a farmer who had come to town seeking a lawyer to defend him in a case about to be heard in court and, who after one look at Marshall's rough clothing had hunted for a more impressively dressed attorney. The countryman had paid his advocate with the powdered wig and foppish clothes a large advance fee, but while he sat in court waiting for his own case to come up his lawyer lost another case to Marshall.

The farmer listened to his man pour out grandiloquent phrases in a pompous manner, then heard Marshall's plain and direct statement of facts and his keen use of logic in totally demolishing the fancy lawyer's argument. He fired his own lawyer on the spot and rushed up to Marshall to explain the situation. The farmer had paid the other lawyer so much he had only five dollars left, but he begged Marshall to take the case. "You didn't look to me like you knew anything," the farmer admitted, "wearing clothes poorer than mine."

Marshall roared with laughter, accepted the fee, and won the case, according to the story. Whether true or not, it was a tale that had Richmond's affectionate approval. Some of Marshall's court victories already were becoming legend. He might not have the manner or learning of other lawyers, but he won cases. Marshall went straight to the core of an argument and reduced it to simple terms the judges could understand without wading through a lot of fussy legal technicalities.

Against the intricate pleadings of those who indulged in flashy flights of oratory, he simply appealed to common sense. His ability to make himself understood by any average citizen in the courtroom won him clients as well as cases. Marshall's courtroom dignity grew somewhat with success, but he never did put on a powdered wig, and his greatness grew from the plain man who could speak and write so a nation would understand.

5

J OHN MARSHALL's first big law case, before the Virginia Court of Appeals, was in the spring of 1786. He represented some fifty-seven clients including George Washington who owned land that got its title from the old Fairfax grants of the British Crown. Marshall lost the case that was directly before the court, as he knew he would, but he gained the much greater legal victory that he sought. He also gained the additional recognition that put him at the very top of his profession as a lawyer.

On the surface, the suit was by the heirs of certain land-owners to make the Fairfax heirs live up to old agreements. There was little doubt that the claimants were entitled to the land in question. Virginia's Attorney General Edmund Randolph joined in the suit to get it for them.

But in the background were years of legal compromise, acts of Assembly, and previous court decisions. There was also the long-standing and bitter resentment of many Virginians against the Fairfax title holders. That dated back to the original grants by the kings of England of more than five million acres. Much of the land had been taken over by colonists through the years under various deeds, claims, Revolutionary War seizures, and by just squatting on it. The whole Fairfax title had long been in dispute and upon it rested the title to a good part of the land in Virginia.

Marshall's main purpose in battling Randolph through three days of court arguments was not to fight over the particular parcel of land being sued for, since he realized that decision was bound to go against him. What he wanted to do was prevent the kind of a decision that might upset the entire Fairfax title. That was far more important to the owners who originally derived their holdings from Lord Fairfax. Marshall made the validity of the basic Fairfax title the center of his argument, kept the court from attacking that, and put it beyond immediate legal dispute.

Aside from the interest of his clients, he had a personal interest, since the Fauquier County lands he and his father owned were based on the Fairfax title, and he soon was to become a major investor in buying up much of the remaining Fairfax grants. Marshall not only won his point but won Randolph's admiration for the legal reasoning he used against him in court. When Randolph was elected Governor of Virginia by the legislature that fall his position meant he no longer would be able to practice law privately and he announced: "I beg leave to inform my clients that John Marshall, Esq., will succeed to my business."

The law business Randolph put in Marshall's hands was one of the best in Richmond. Added to Marshall's own, it meant he could just about pick and choose the cases he wanted to handle. He was chosen by men of wealth and large affairs to watch over their interests, became the lawyer in Richmond for other prominent lawyers around the state, and before long was recognized as an authority on business and property law.

But despite his prosperity, Marshall was a deeply troubled man. He was convinced that the new nation which had been born of such suffering and such exalted hope was falling apart and that unless something was done to save it the dream of the United States would die. He had watched with hope when the newly independent and sovereign states finally agreed to form a "firm league of friendship" under the Articles of Confederation, but instead of achieving their announced "permanent union," the states were acting toward one another like a group of quarreling foreign nations, more at odds than they were united. American government seemed to him like a driverless wagon hitched to thirteen horses, all pulling at once in different directions and headed only for calamity.

Congress could levy no taxes. It could make few demands of any sort that the states were compelled to honor. There were no general courts for the settlement of disputes among the states. Each state treated outsiders as foreigners. The states jealously passed tariff and trade restrictions against one another, refused to honor contracts and debts, and could offer no real protection of person or property. Some states printed as much paper currency as they pleased, which led to inflation; others rejected that temptation and their angry citizens threatened insurrection. The currency of one state was heavily discounted in the next. A maze of conflicting legal barriers stood in the way of free trade among the states and also made it hard for merchants to collect for goods that had been sold or for bankers to collect their loans, which severely limited credit and investment.

Conditions finally became so impossible that a convention was called in Annapolis in September, 1786, to talk over interstate problems and consider adopting uniform commercial regulations. Marshall knew from Madison, who went as a delegate from Virginia, that he and Washington, along with Alexander Hamilton of New York and others, hoped to bring about a real reform of the Articles of Confederation. But delegates from only five of the states bothered to turn up at the Annapolis meeting, so there was little they could accomplish. They did ask Congress to call for another convention to meet in Philadelphia in May, 1787. Marshall wrote that "Madison was the parent of the resolution for appointing members of a general convention to be held in Philadelphia for the purpose of revising the Confederation."

Congress, in agreeing to the call, limited the powers of the Philadelphia meeting "to the sole and express purpose of revising the Articles of Confederation." But Marshall, who had been working closely with Madison in Virginia, was convinced revision wasn't enough. Some entirely new form of government was needed, a strong national government controlled by men of excellence and established leadership, to expand prosperity at home and give America honor and standing in the world.

Under the Confederation, America's word, like its credit, could not be depended upon. Its diplomats could make only fumbling attempts to reach international agreements, knowing that anything agreed upon might be ignored by the states. The new country was surrounded by the colonies of European nations and its weakness invited threats to divide or destroy.

Most Americans had no greater fear than that they might be ruled by some far-distant central government beyond their direct reach and control. They had sacrificed, fought and died to keep from paying taxes to far-off British kings and were fiercely determined to preserve their hard-won liberties to live as they pleased without any government to tell them what they must do. In near-poverty, illiterate, ill-informed, isolated in small communities, easily swayed by emotional appeals to fear and ignorance, deeply suspicious of all authority, great masses of the people hardly thought of themselves as belonging to any nation. Their interests were bounded by their farms and towns, or at most by their states.

Marshall's fear was different. He, too, had fought for liberty, but not individual license to ignore responsible authority.

He wanted a government for all the people, not one pulled apart by selfish local interests of separate states. As a man of property, conservative views, business and family connections with those of wealth and position, he had less faith in rebellious mass rule than in a government well-run by capable leaders, selected by the consent of the whole nation from among those best qualified. The term was not yet generally used, but he had become a confirmed Federalist.

As the time for the Philadelphia convention neared, he and others who shared similar views were alarmed by a people's uprising in Massachusetts that seemed proof of their worst fears. Hundreds of farmers, war veterans, and others had been thrown into jail in Massachusetts when they were unable to pay their debts. When the state refused demands to issue paper money freely to ease financial hardships and also rejected their appeals for relief, people began to hold mass protest meetings against the government and to stage demonstrations that often turned to mob violence. Mobs of desperate poverty-driven people in several western Massachusetts towns prevented the courts from sitting, smashed open jails and released prisoners, and attacked personal property and individuals.

The uprisings became a full rebellion under the leadership of Revolutionary War veteran Daniel Shays. With six hundred followers, armed with their old war muskets, he broke up a session of the state Superior Court at Springfield. Shays' forces grew to some two thousand men. Governor James Bowdoin called out the militia. When Shays' "people's army" marched into Springfield in an attempt to seize the arsenal, an overwhelming force of state troops defeated them in a brief battle.

The Massachusetts' rebellion was soon ended and order restored throughout the state, but while it lasted the uprising thoroughly frightened conservative public leaders. Washington wrote Madison that he feared "we are fast verging to anarchy." Marshall wrote a friend that "all is gloom" and that whatever the cause of the uprisings "they deeply affect the happiness and reputation of the United States" and that "we may live to see another revolution." They had cast "a deep shade," Marshall thought, "over that bright prospect which . . . the establishment of our free government had opened to the votaries of liberty throughout the globe."

Thomas Jefferson, far away in Paris as America's minister to France, shared none of their alarm. Jefferson was telling French friends that the American government in which the states kept all the power under the Confederation was "without comparison the best existing or that ever did exist." He was, as he put it, "not a friend to a very energetic government" although he agreed that the Articles of Confederation should be strengthened in regard to trade with foreign nations. He had begun to sympathize with the start of the movement that was to lead to the French Revolution, and in him the fires of individual liberty burned more brightly than those of Federal control.

When word reached Jefferson in Paris of Shays' Rebellion in Massachusetts, he wrote: "The spirit of resistance to government is so valuable on certain occasions that I wish it to be always kept alive. It will often be exercised when wrong, but better so than not to be exercised at all. I like a little rebellion now and then. It is like a storm in the atmosphere." His advice from Paris to the delegates who were meeting in Philadelphia to revise the Articles of Confederation was: "Make the states one as to everything connected with foreign nations, and several as to everything purely domestic."

But most of the delegates to the Philadelphia convention in May, 1787, were determined to do far more than revise the old Confederation, even though Congress had limited their power to that. Their determination was stiffened by Shays' Rebellion. Although nineteen of the appointed delegates failed to attend, some fifty-five others, with Washington presiding, debated for four hundred hours through the hot and humid Philadelphia summer in the plain red brick building which had been the birthplace of the Declaration of Independence. With armed guards at the door, and pledged to the strictest secrecy to keep the public from learning what they were doing, they overthrew the existing government and produced by peaceful revolution what history was to know as the Constitution of the United States.

Virginia's delegates, headed by Governor Randolph and including Madison and George Mason, the father of Virginia's own state constitution, had arrived at the convention before most of the others. While they were waiting for the convention to start, they held their own meetings and worked out a plan of government, based mostly on Madison's ideas, which Randolph presented. Many other ideas and compromises finally produced the Constitution, but much of its basic framework was built upon Madison's suggestions.

Randolph and Mason, however, objected so strongly to the broad and implied powers granted Congress in the final document that they refused to sign it. Fourteen other delegates also refused to sign. But thirty-nine delegates, representing all the states but Rhode Island, which wanted no part in the affair and had not sent representatives to the meeting, put their names to the Constitution. Many considered it far from perfect, but better than nothing, and the real battle to get the sovereign states to ratify the "new plan" of national government began.

Marshall had no real desire to return to public office. His law work kept him as busy as he wanted to be and he no longer needed the added prestige that his earlier place in the legislature had given him. But the Federalists needed him to help put Virginia in line for the Constitution. Washington, in letters from his home in Mount Vernon, was urging a careful campaign to win ratification, and Madison was leading the fight in Virginia, but they had no direct voice in the legislature.

Marshall needed little urging to become that voice. "Though devoted to my profession," as he explained, he entered the 1787 election contest "with a good deal of spirit." For the third time, he was elected a member of the legislature, and the fall session was only three days old when Virginia's first fight over the Constitution began.

The immediate question before the legislature was not whether to approve the "new plan" of government, but whether to let Virginia consider it at all. Members hardly knew what was in the proposed Constitution, since it had just been delivered to them. Federalists wanted the legislature to call a state convention of delegates who would be limited either to accepting or rejecting the Constitution outright. Opponents knew they had little chance of blocking the convention call, but their strategy was to delay action by demanding that convention delegates be given the right in advance to offer amendments to the Constitution before any vote was taken to ratify it.

Patrick Henry, the veteran champion of the people's liberties, led the opponents. His strongest argument was that the Constitution lacked a Bill of Rights. Many who sided with him charged that the new government was designed to benefit wealthy aristocrats, that it meant supreme power for the rich and only taxes and restrictions for the poor, and that it was worded to limit the direct will of the majority.

Virginia's decision, as the nation's biggest state, was crucial because of the effect it would have on other states where ratification battles were underway. If Virginia hesitated over calling a convention to consider the Constitution, or managed to attach prior amendments, other states also might delay. Amendments by one state would have to be submitted for approval by all the others and ratification could be dragged out endlessly. Those against the Constitution hoped that if they stalled long enough the whole plan would collapse.

Marshall and the Virginia Federalists were fighting first of all to get the legislature to act and to get the state convention started. But hostility to the Constitution grew and the legislature became deadlocked. After the heated debate had gone on for days, Marshall stepped in to offer a compromise. He said that he wasn't satisfied with the arguments on either side, but that both had some merit, and that the solution was to put the question directly to the people.

He appealed to the legislature not to take a stand on the proposed Constitution before the people themselves had even elected a convention to act on it. The question should go to the people without prejudice, he said, and he proposed his own resolution that "a convention should be called and that the new Constitution should be laid before them for their free and ample discussion."

It was a plan that soothed both factions and pleased almost everybody. Federalists were convinced they could carry the Constitution through such a convention without having amendments attached. Patrick Henry and his friends were equally sure they would be able to amend or defeat it in the convention. Both sides thought they had won by avoiding an immediate and uncertain showdown in the legislature.

Marshall, in effect, let everybody have his own way and succeeded in his major purpose of getting a state convention called. His resolution passed the House without a single vote against it, and although the state Senate argued for several weeks before agreeing, the call was issued for a convention with no strings attached. Copies of Marshall's resolution were sent to the national Congress and to the governors and legislatures of other states to inform them of Virginia's action. The state convention was set for June, 1788, and the election of delegates got underway.

Most Virginians were against quick ratification of the Constitution and Richmond's Henrico County was a hotbed of opposition. The people were certain to elect their handsome and popular Governor Randolph as one of the county's delegates. Washington, Madison and other Federalist leaders decided Marshall was the only man they had a chance of electing as the county's second delegate. His Federalist views were well-known, but he hadn't aroused the people against him by being belligerent about them. He was well-liked, had done a lot for Richmond in community projects, and probably had more friends than anyone else in the county.

His opponent was one of the physicians who treated Polly, Dr. William Foushee, an outright supporter of Patrick Henry's stand against the Constitution. Many people sided with his views but didn't like him much personally. Randolph described Foushee as "a perfect Henryite" but doubted that he was "popular enough on other scores to be elected."

Randolph himself was being won over to full support of the Constitution. Most Richmond voters took it for granted that Randolph was against the Constitution because he had refused to sign it, but he actually approved its main features although he thought it had serious defects. Washington and others appealed to Randolph to change his stand and in flattering letters Washington told him he was the one man who had it in his power to save the Union. While the election of Virginia convention delegates was underway, Randolph quietly began working with the Federalists. He was overwhelmingly elected by those who expected him to fight the Constitution.

Marshall's contest was closer but when the votes were counted he also had a majority. He had won, not because of his views, but despite them. "The county," Marshall later wrote, "was decidedly Anti-Federal, but I was at that time popular, and parties had not yet become so bitter as to extinguish the private affections."

Both he and Randolph, who would fight for the Constitution, were chosen delegates by voters who were mostly against the Constitution. Much the same thing happened in other counties where Federalists put up personally popular candidates. Most Virginians didn't want the proposed new national government, but really knew little about it and were inclined to let men they had always admired as leaders come to a decision for them.

Marshall was taken into the inner councils of the Federalists and from daily discussions with Madison, Randolph and others gained lasting knowledge not only of the written provisions of the Constitution but of the aims and intentions of those who had written it. The Virginia convention itself would furnish the first full and open debate and examination of the Constitution, article by article and clause by clause, and Marshall's part in it gave him an education in the basic law of the land few other men had.

Even in those beginning days of the nation, as forever afterwards, much of the really decisive political maneuvering was behind the scenes. Federalists and their opponents began active lobbying for votes and influence long before the convention started. Marshall used his personal charm and fellowship to good effect, winning friends for the Constitution. As a lobbyist, he was one of the best the Virginia Federalists had. He wined and dined arriving delegates, helped see to their personal comfort and accommodation, and made sure Richmond provided a gracious welcome. He and Polly had just become parents of their second son, named Jacquelin after her father, but the happy event didn't interfere with their home entertaining of those whose political favors might be gained. Their dinner parties were frequent and sometimes lavish, as Marshall's account book showed.

Robert Morris of Philadelphia, probably the richest man in America, was among influential Federalists from other parts of the country who came to Virginia to help with the lobbying and he was often among guests at the Marshall home, with his wife and two daughters. Long a patriot leader, Morris had given his services and his money unstintingly to the cause of the Constitution, and as one of its signers he had put his power behind its ratification in Pennsylvania.

Morris also had come to Richmond because he had extensive business interests in Virginia that Marshall looked after as his attorney. There were other bonds between Marshall and the wealthy Philadelphian. Both shared an admiration for the views of Alexander Hamilton, whose Federalist writings made such an impression on Marshall they were to be reflected in some of his later Court opinions. Marshall's younger brother James had been a lieutenant in Hamilton's regiment at the battle of Yorktown, had become a favorite of Hamilton's, and was serving Hamilton's interests in the preconvention political maneuverings in Richmond. James Marshall also had begun to take a personal interest in one of Morris's daughters, the lovely Hester Morris. She later would become his wife and thus link the Morris and Marshall families through marriage.

While Virginia was waiting to hold its convention, the battles for ratification went on in other states. The approval of nine states was needed and eight had voted for the Constitution by the time the Virginia delegates met in June, 1788. The ninth and deciding state was to be New Hampshire, which gave its approval four days before the Virginia convention finally reached its decision, but the delayed news of New Hampshire's action didn't reach the other states until the real crisis was over.

The fate of the new government rested on what would be done in Virginia and New York, because without them there could be no effective Union even if all the other states approved. New York was known to be strongly against the

Constitution and the greatest hope of turning the tide there lay in the influence that a victory in Virginia would have on the New Yorkers. For his own state, but far more to decide whether there was to be a firm nation of United States, Marshall took up the battle for "a well-regulated democracy" as the "best means of protecting liberty."

6

PEOPLE SWARMED into Richmond in June, 1788, to fill every bed, bunk and stable in town. Some were seriously concerned about the fate of government but others came just for fun. The battle over the Constitution had to compete with the lure of the race track, since Richmond's annual Jockey Club races started at the same time. When Patrick Henry or some other favorite spoke, people jammed the galleries of the New Academy Building where the convention was held, but when lesser debaters took to the floor the race track drew the crowd away.

Virginia's 170 delegates included lawyers, doctors, clergymen, farmers and Indian fighters, young and old, ignorant and educated, but all leaders in the districts from which they came. Many had never read the Constitution they were to vote on, but the general idea had filtered through to everybody that the issue was whether to establish a supreme central government over the states.

The Virginians were fully aware that their convention would be a sounding board that would echo loudly in the other states. Alexander Hamilton, commanding the desperate ratification fight in New York, sent word to Madison that "If you do

well, there is a gleam of hope; but certainly I think not otherwise. . . . God grant that Virginia may accede. The example
will have a vast influence."

George Washington, the guiding spirit of the Constitution,
wasn't in Richmond, but special couriers kept him informed
of every development and he sent frequent messages of advice. Madison was the convention floor manager for the
Federalists. They did so well lining up delegate support in
advance that they quickly put their own men in charge of
the convention and captured parliamentary control that helped
them carry their well-organized strategy through three weeks
of debate.

Unanimously chosen President of the Convention was aged
Judge Edmund Pendleton. Marshall's law professor during
his brief stay at William and Mary, George Wythe, was made
Chairman of the Committee of the Whole, and Marshall himself was put on a committee to examine delegate election
returns and to decide the seating of contested delegates.

Madison, though unimpressive physically and a poor public
speaker, was ready to bring his brilliant mind to the debates
over the Constitution he had greatly helped to write. Governor
Randolph was waiting to throw his bombshell by announcing
his full support of it. Also in the Federalist arsenal of speakers
were the oratorical fat man George Nicholas, the equally giant
James Innes, considered only second to Patrick Henry as Virginia's greatest public speaker, and the dashing cavalry hero
of the Revolution, Light-Horse Harry Lee.

Leading the opposition, Patrick Henry was still the man of
golden tongue and mighty vocal thunder. He had lost the
vigor of youth, was stooped and prematurely old at fifty-two,
had to squint through spectacles because of fading eyesight,
and had trouble keeping his wig from bouncing crookedly on
his balding head when he was in the fury of debate, but
his mind had lost none of its cunning, his words still cast a

spell, and he remained the people's idol. Backing Henry, opponents of the Constitution had venerable George Mason ready to explain why he had refused to sign it, aristocratic former Governor Benjamin Harrison, Oxford-educated William Grayson, and Marshall's own friend, James Monroe.

Marshall took no part in the first ten days of debate. Henry, Madison, Randolph, Mason, Pendleton and Nicholas, the leaders of the convention, some of them talking five hours at a stretch, had all made their first arguments before Marshall was called into it. His friend Monroe had just spoken against the Constitution, warning against "this haste . . . this wild precipitation" to overthrow the old Confederation for "a dangerous new government."

For the occasion of his first major public address, Marshall was wearing a new coat Polly had talked him into buying. His voice was rather thin and dry and he was no emotional orator, but what he said was persuasive and to the point. "We, sir, idolize democracy," he said in answer to the charge that the Constitution would destroy it. "We prefer this system . . . because we are convinced that it has a greater tendency to secure our liberty and promote our happiness. We admire it because we think it a well-regulated democracy." The principles of good government, he said, were "a strict observance of justice and public faith" and if those principles had been observed under the old Confederation "the friends of liberty would not be so willing now to part with it."

Henry and others had raised the warning that Congress could not be trusted to make laws or a President to make treaties since they would be too far removed from the will of the people. But Marshall said, "You cannot exercise the powers of government personally yourselves. You must trust to agents." Refusing to trust in the elected officials of government because there was a chance they might abuse their power could lead only to anarchy, he went on, saying that "if you repose no confidence in delegates, because there is a possibility of their abusing it, you can have no government; for the power of doing good is inseparable from that of doing some evil."

Members of Congress would be as accountable for their conduct as members of Virginia's own legislature, and to be re-elected it would be "necessary for them to confer with the people," so it would be against their own interest to abuse their power. "It is the people that give power, and can take it back," Marshall said. "They are the masters who give it, and of whom their servants hold it. . . . The government is not supported by force, but depending on our own free will."

Henry, as well as Mason and Monroe, had attacked the power that the new Congress would have to levy taxes, warning that a tax-hungry national government would send its revenue agents out over the land as "unfeeling blood-suckers" who would delight in searching every home and barn to seize the property of poor debtors. Henry had raged that the people would be no better off than the colonies had been under hated British rule and that in fact they might be far safer with a monarchy than with the government of the Constitution.

Marshall's answer to that was: "We were *not* represented in Parliament. Here we are represented." The Constitution's choice, he said, was between "democracy or despotism," not by embracing the system of the English kings, but by choosing a system "where the people hold all the powers in their own hands, and delegate them cautiously, for short periods, to their servants, who are accountable for the smallest mal-administrations." He called the power of taxation "essentially necessary, for without it there will be no efficiency in the government," and said the Confederation had proved taxes could not be properly collected by begging the states. "We have had a sufficient demonstration of the vanity of depending on requisitions. . . . The Confederation has nominal powers but no means to carry them into effect."

He ranged over almost all the objections the Constitution's opponents had made, but the Federalists' main battle was to block the demand for amendments before ratifying the Constitution and on that Marshall said: "There are in this state and in every state of the Union many who are enemies of the Union. They will bring amendments . . . which they know will not be accepted. . . . Disunion will be their object." If the states hoped to get together to make friendly and mutual concessions, then amendments should wait until after the new government was formed, he said, because "until we have experience on the subject, amendments as well as the Constitution itself are to try. Let us try it, and keep our hands free to change it when necessary."

Marshall's speech was well-received, but seemed to have little effect in changing delegate votes. At the end of the second week's debate Madison sent word to Washington that "the business is in the most ticklish state that can be imagined." He wrote: "The majority will certainly be very small on whatever side it may finally lie; and I dare not encourage much expectation that it will be on the favorable side."

When the delegates took their seats again after a weekend recess, Henry launched into a tirade against the proposed powers of the President, the creation of a standing army, and the fact that the new Federal capital would be outside the boundaries of any state's control. He painted a terrifying word picture of the President as a future tyrant who could use the Federal district as a fortified camp from which to send troops to raid the unprotected countryside and to plunder and to kill.

Marshall took to the floor to ridicule Henry's statements as wild exaggeration. The states would still have their own militias, he said, but if war should come and the government

was without a strong national army, "state after state will
fall and will be a sacrifice to the want of power in the Federal
government." The problems of defense during the Revolution
had made it only too clear that "it requires a superintending
power ... to call forth the resources of all to protect all."

While Marshall's voice was important, Madison and others
carried the burden of the early debates. But when the convention reached its climax with a lengthy debate over the
proposed Federal court system, the floor leaders chose Marshall to make the main defense of the Constitution.

The choice was made not because they recognized in him
any budding genius of judicial understanding, since Wythe,
Pendleton, Innes, and Randolph all had far more experience
at the bench and bar than Marshall, but because it was the
final battle to win votes and they decided his personality would
count most. The majority of delegates were plain people and
he was a man who could speak plain truths and discuss the
deadly dry subject of the judiciary in simple non-technical
terms the delegates would understand.

Opponents led off the debate over the courts. Mason charged
the new national judiciary was constructed to "destroy the
dearest rights of the community" and to "destroy state governments." Henry pulled out all the emotional stops in playing
upon the fears of his listeners. "The purse is gone, the sword
is gone," he cried, "and now the scales of justice are to be
given away." Men would be dragged from their homes and
taken across the country to far-distant Federal courts where
they would stand defenseless among strangers and before
tyrant judges, Henry warned, and the Federal government
would spread limitless courts of its own into every state and
district to challenge the authority of state courts and to try
men for their very lives in denial of their sacred right to be
judged by juries of their neighbors.

Marshall's main task in taking on the two champions of

the opposition was to quiet the fears Mason and Henry had so vividly aroused. He deliberately spoke gently, calmly, without emotion. But there were passages of eloquence in what he said, and others that foreshadowed the great Constitutional decisions he was to make in years to come.

The new Federal courts would be "a great improvement on that system from which we are now departing," Marshall said, because they would be "tribunals appointed for the decision of controversies which were before either not at all, or improperly, provided for." There was no reason to assume that national courts would not be as fair as state courts. "What is it that makes us trust our judges?" he asked, and answered, "Their independence in office and manner of appointment." Federal judges would be "equally if not more independent" and certainly there was "as much wisdom and knowledge in the United States as in a particular state" for the choice of judges.

He made gentle fun of his opponents for contradicting their own arguments when they said on one hand that men might be dragged across the country for trial in some distant place, and warned on the other hand that Congress might put courts into every district. Marshall said they couldn't have it both ways. As for himself, he thought it wise to let Congress create secondary courts wherever it might prove necessary to "remove the inconvenience of being dragged to the centre of the United States." He called it absurd to argue that Federal courts would extend their power to cover all cases handled by state courts. "The state courts would not lose the jurisdiction of the causes they now decide," he said, since Federal courts would be restricted to "cases arising under the Constitution and laws of the United States."

Marshall then stated the doctrine he was to announce years later from the Supreme Court bench in his historic decisions that the Court had the right to rule laws of Congress unconstitutional. He asked the Virginia convention, "Has the government of the United States power to make laws on every subject? Can they go beyond the delegated powers?"

His answer was: "If they were to make a law not warranted by any of the powers enumerated, it would be considered by the judges as an infringement of the Constitution which they are to guard. They would not consider such a law as coming under their jurisdiction. They would declare it void." And he asked, "To what quarter will you look for protection from an infringement on the Constitution, if you will not give that power to the judiciary? There is no other body that can afford such a protection."

Marshall spoke at length about suits in national courts between citizens of different states, disputes among the states themselves, and between states and foreign nations, and expressed the belief that having courts which could settle such controversies would bring added justice and "help preserve peace." But he made one statement that was to plague him later when his Supreme Court opinions took a different view. "I hope that no gentleman will think that a state will be called at the bar of the Federal court," he said. "It is not rational to suppose that the sovereign power should be dragged before a court."

As Virginia's great battle neared its end, Madison sent worried messages to Hamilton in New York. He thought Virginia's decision might hang on as few as three or four votes. Both sides were desperate and off-the-floor lobbying became intense. The Constitution's opponents talked of forcing an adjournment, of walking out of the convention to block a decision, and tried to arouse fresh fears by warning that if the Constitution were ratified without prior amendment the people would riot and rise in rebellion.

Federalists took an unofficial delegate poll and decided ratification without some kind of amendment would be impossible. But they still wanted the Constitution adopted without prior strings attached. Henry and his followers were ready to propose amendments, so the Federalists quickly stepped in with a compromise of their own, before Henry could take the floor. Wythe announced that the Federalists would make amendments themselves. But they would be made only as recommendations to Congress, and only after ratification had been completed, not before.

When Henry finally got a chance to talk he was enraged. He accused the Federalists of unfair tactics, charged them with trying to railroad the Constitution through even though they themselves now admitted it had "capital defects." Nine-tenths of Virginia's people were against it, Henry declared, and so were people in states where it had already been ratified under "illegal pressure."

Henry warned, in what was to be almost the last great public speech of his life, that the Constitution was filled with "an awful immensity of dangers," and that as it stood he would have "nothing to do with it." He offered a Bill of Rights he had drawn himself and vowed that he and his followers would never consent to adoption without it. "Our own happiness alone is not affected by the event," he said. "All nations are interested in the determination. . . . We have it in our power to secure the happiness of one-half of the human race. Its adoption may involve the misery of the other hemisphere."

As Patrick Henry thundered on, a furious summer storm suddenly struck to bring nature's drama to his own. The full day darkened and there was a howling wind. Great flashes of lightning crackled through the hall and its walls shook to rolls of thunder. Henry spoke on through it, but some delegates fled the building to seek more substantial cover. Up on the hill in the Marshall home, Polly was so frightened by the storm that she gathered her sons and hid under a blanket with them.

The showdown was put off until the next day, and finally the vote came. Henry's resolution for prior amendments was beaten down. Wythe's resolution, promising to grant almost all the amendments opponents wanted in the form of recommendations after the Constitution was ratified, won. With that out of the way, the vote was taken on the Constitution itself. A few delegates refused to vote at all and some others voted for the Constitution despite positive instructions from their districts to vote against it. The Constitution was saved in Virginia by only ten votes. It was ratified 89 to 79.

Henry admitted his defeat. He told the delegates that "though overpowered in a good cause, yet will I be a peaceable citizen." He would yield his sword to the victors, the old patriot said, and would work only in "a constitutional way" to "remove the defects" of the Constitution. He would lead no walkout from the hall.

When the Constitution's wrathful opponents later held a night mass meeting to arouse a public demonstration, Henry appeared before them to quiet the furious gathering. He had done his best against the Constitution, he told them, but had done it "in the proper place." The question was settled, he said, and advised them "as true and faithful republicans" to halt their demonstration and go home.

Marshall was chosen a member of two committees appointed to carry out the promise to recommend possible amendments to Congress. The convention finally adopted some twenty amendments and twenty more articles of rights that closely followed what Henry had suggested. The Virginia amendments were much stronger than those which were eventually adopted by Congress, but along with the recommendations from other states they formed a foundation for the Bill of Rights that later became the first ten amendments to the Constitution.

Belated news came of New Hampshire's ratification and early in July the old Congress of Confederation, announcing that the Constitution had been adopted, set up elections for the new government and quietly prepared to pass out of existence. New York, after a desperate struggle won by Hamilton, soon joined the Union.

George Washington, as everybody expected, was elected first President, with John Adams of Massachusetts as Vice-President. Washington rewarded Edmund Randolph for his services in the Virginia convention by making him Attorney General. Hamilton became Secretary of the Treasury, and the absent Jefferson was called back from France to become Secretary of State. John Marshall returned for a time to the Virginia legislature and to his private practice of law.

JOHN MARSHALL knew the Constitution had not made a
new government. It was a blueprint for government, but
whether it would work and whether the people would accept
it was far from certain. The battles in the states over its
adoption had widened a deep division of the American people.
President Washington's cabinet became the first battleground,
with Alexander Hamilton and Thomas Jefferson fighting each
other like what Jefferson called "cocks in a pit" over their
opposite political theories.

Marshall became Washington's chief defender in Virginia
as all America began to take sides in what eventually would
grow into the first two political parties. As Washington's champion and an advocate of Hamilton's financial policies, Marshall became Jefferson's enemy. He turned down an offer by
Washington to appoint him Virginia's Federal district attorney,
but did seek and win re-election to the state legislature from
Richmond in 1789, and there found himself once again battling Patrick Henry in a fight that was part of the bigger one
between the Jeffersonians and the Federalists. It started over
the nation's money troubles.

The United States began with a fifty-two million dollar

debt, owed for bonds and warrants issued by the old Continental Congress. Plus that, the various states had issued securities for about eighteen million dollars more to raise war funds, and little of it had been paid. Hamilton, to get the country off to a sound financial start, asked the new Congress to approve payment of the entire debt, national and state, at full face value by the government. Congress agreed to pay what the nation owed, but balked at paying what the states owed, with Jefferson's followers leading the opposition to that half of Hamilton's plan.

Marshall fully agreed with Hamilton's view that the states had all gone into debt for a common cause and that the money they owed was the nation's "price of liberty." But those who sided with Jefferson believed it was an unconstitutional invasion of states' rights and a scheme to rob the poor and reward the rich because most of the old soldiers and others who originally held government warrants and securities had long since sold them at depression prices to speculators who now would gain full face value.

Patrick Henry's Virginians had a particular cause for fury. Virginia had already paid off its war debts through tax hardships and the sale of public lands. Most Virginians saw no reason why they should have to pay again, through the national government, by sharing a tax burden with other states that had failed to meet their own debts. It was hard to convince them that the financial standing and credit of the new Union depended upon all states working together to wipe out the old debts.

The battle in the national Congress ended when the two cabinet enemies, Hamilton and Jefferson, made a private deal. Jefferson agreed to swing enough Southern votes to ease Hamilton's debt payment plan through Congress in exchange for Hamilton's trade of Northern votes to establish the proposed new "Federal City" at a site on the Potomac River.

It was a great victory for the Federalists and Hamilton's program sailed through Congress to put the nation on a firm financial footing. It also put some forty million dollars into the pockets of speculators, and Jefferson soon was crying that he had been "tricked."

When news of what Congress had done reached Virginia, the legislature exploded. Marshall, as a leading Federalist spokesman, caught the full blast. Patrick Henry drew up a resolution for the State of Virginia to censure Congress and "sound the alarm" for the American people to defend their rights against an invasion of "unbounded influence, which pervading every branch of the government, bears down all opposition and daily threatens the destruction of . . . liberty."

Marshall's attempt to defeat the resolution was angrily rejected. Virginia went on record with a stinging rebuke to Congress that amounted to a Magna Charta of states' rights. It accused the Federalists of trying to "erect, concentrate and perpetuate a large monied interest" to prostrate "agriculture at the feet of commerce" and to produce a government "fatal to the existence of American liberty."

It was the first formal call to battle for the doctrine that all powers not expressly given in the Constitution were reserved to the states. For the nation to assume the state debts, it declared, was not "warranted by the Constitution of the United States . . . and is repugnant to an express provision of that Constitution."

When Hamilton read the Virginia resolution, he said: "This is the first symptom of a spirit which must either be killed, or will kill the Constitution of the United States."

But Jefferson oppositely believed that to "take a single step beyond the boundaries . . . drawn around the powers of Congress is to take possession of a boundless field of power, no longer susceptible to any definition."

Jefferson by then was leading a fight against Hamilton's

plan to establish a Bank of the United States and their enmity over that and other things before very long would drive Jefferson to resign from the cabinet. He also had made a political alliance with Madison, who would lead his battles in Congress. Out of the conflicts would come Jefferson's new party of opposition, a party of the common men, for states' rights and individual liberties and against men of wealth, aristocracy and Federalism.

To Marshall and the Federalists, the Jeffersonian movement was an uprising of radicals against the still weak national government. The Constitution had not been planned for a two-party system and Federalists felt it was "illegal and immoral" to divide the country into rival political factions.

Marshall quit the legislature at the end of the term, driven out by the Anti-Federalist tide. Hamilton wanted him to run for the national Congress and when Jefferson heard the rumors he suggested to Madison that a way to keep Marshall out of Congress might be to sidetrack him with some other position. "I think nothing better could be done," Jefferson wrote, "than to make him a judge."

But Marshall had no desire then to be either a judge or a Congressman, since his law practice was the best in the state and he had no intention of giving up the income from it. Although he was out of the legislature for a time, he was not silenced. As Washington started his unhappy second term as President in 1793, Marshall remained his strongest and most outspoken supporter in Virginia.

The French Revolution did as much as domestic quarrels to divide America politically. America was caught up in an emotional frenzy of delight over the rebellion of the French people against their king, partly inspired by America's own previous revolution against a British king. For many, it symbolized their own feelings of rebellion against the controls of the new Federal government. But as French radicals turned to mob rule and the gutters of Paris ran with the blood of Royalists, Marshall and other conservatives took a dimmer view of what was happening in France and he began to speak out against the rise of related passions at home.

France put fresh fuel beneath the boiling American political pot by declaring war against the British Empire and by sending Edmond Genêt as its minister to the United States to win America's support. Many expected that America, grateful for the Revolutionary War help the French had given, and still in military alliance with France, would rush to arms to defend France against England.

Marshall won no popularity by pointing out that it was the beheaded French monarch, not the French revolutionists, who had sent help to America when it was most needed. More important, he argued, was the fact that the weak United States was in no position to become involved in any foreign war. Those had been Washington's views and the President put them into a proclamation of American neutrality.

But most Americans were for France and for the Revolution. Marshall, for the first time in his life, learned what it was to have a full storm of public emotion against him. Those who had always been against strong government of any kind identified the French Revolution with their own cause and that of states' rights. When Marshall continued to speak in support of neutrality and the need for loyalty to the Federal government, he was attacked as an enemy of France and of Republican freedoms by the Jeffersonians who were starting to call themselves Republicans.

Citizen Genêt, the young and handsome new French minister, had landed at Charleston as American neutrality was proclaimed and had decided to ignore both the law and the President, and to go over Washington's head with a direct appeal to the American people to join France and fight England. As he made his slow trip northward toward the capital in Philadelphia, there were dinners, parades, mass meetings and cheering celebrations. Women showered him with flowers, children were taught French songs to sing him, and French fever spread over the East.

Americans donned Liberty Caps, staged mock beheadings of Louis XVI, took to calling each other "Citizen" and "Citizeness." In their desire to have done with all trappings of authority, some refused to call a clergyman "Reverend," or to speak of a judge as "His Honor." Overwhelmed by such adulation, Citizen Genêt began to swear American citizens to an oath of allegiance to France, to hire soldiers, outfit French fighting ships in American ports, and set up his own French courts on American soil.

Marshall watched it all with alarm and urged Virginians not to be taken in by what he called a "malignant philosophy." He considered the most dangerous of Genêt's activities the encouraging of secret political societies that were springing up throughout the country, vowing support for France and the downfall of Federalism. Genêt's own arrogance finally turned public opinion against him when he began insulting Revolutionary War heroes as well as the President, tried to stir up American military action against Canada and Florida, and openly violated the neutrality law by sending privateers sailing out to capture British vessels in American waters.

President Washington demanded his recall as minister and by then Genêt had lost favor with his own changing government in Paris. When an envoy arrived to take him back for beheading, he escaped the guillotine and remained in the United States by becoming an American citizen. The French fever slowly began to subside somewhat, but not the American political passions it had inflamed.

Marshall's Republican enemies denounced not only his political beliefs, but publicly and privately slandered his character, ability, habits, and honesty. A whispering campaign spread lies that he was a confirmed drunkard who spent all his time carousing, gambling, and in company with persons of ill-repute. Stories about him were spread to the highest levels of government. Polly's sister Eliza wrote a relative that "it was cruelly insinuated to George Washington that to Marshall's fondness for play was added an increasing fondness for liquor" and that "slanderous enemies . . . would catch at the most trifling circumstances to throw a shade over his fair name."

Newspapers had grown in number and circulation and few pretended to be impartial. Federalist papers, in words and lurid cartoons, pictured the rising Republicans as mobs of wild cutthroat anarchists consorting with the Devil in the person of Thomas Jefferson. Republican papers ridiculed President Washington as an "ass" in picturing him astride a donkey and also showed him in the robes of a would-be king who hoped to establish an American monarchy with a Federalist court. Some printed gleeful cartoons of the American people leading Washington to the guillotine.

Writers for similar Republican papers in Virginia called Marshall a pretentious upstart with little education, overrated talent, and bad habits who supported Washington's policies only because they were putting large sums of money into his pockets. They charged he was "linked with wicked financial interests" and that his Federalism was "proof of improper motives."

In a letter to Madison, Jefferson himself suggested Marshall was putting on an act of "profound hypocrisy" by adopting casual dress and "lax lounging manners" in an attempt to don the "mask of Republicanism" so as to make "the bulk of the people of Richmond" think he was one of them.

Madison joined the gossipers by writing Jefferson that Marshall was "at the head of the great purchase from Fairfax" and that he had gotten his funds for it from Hamilton's Bank of the United States. According to Madison, the tie-in Marshall had with "the monied interests" was enough to explain his political defense of Hamilton's policies to "everyone that reflects in the active character he is assuming."

The fact that such attacks were based on a grain of truth made them all the more damaging. Marshall and his brother James had decided to form a group to buy some 200,000 acres that were the remainder of the Fairfax estates. But he got no backing from the Bank of the United States. His partner in the deal was his wealthy law client, Robert Morris, who was also about to become his brother's father-in-law. Morris expected to raise the funds from loans negotiated in Europe on his own immense American real estate holdings.

As it turned out, Morris soon was to run into financial difficulties which would leave Marshall in desperate need for money and facing troubles over the Fairfax lands for years to come. But Morris then was still among the nation's richest men and was able to promise all the backing needed for the Fairfax purchase. Marshall was speculating, as he had been in buying other land that he hoped would increase in value, but there was no dishonesty involved.

The personal attacks hurt and sometimes angered Marshall, but what bothered him more was the abuse heaped upon Washington, Hamilton, and others he admired. He wrote a friend: "Seriously there appears to me every day to be more folly, envy, malice and damn rascality in the world than there was the day before and I do verily begin to think that plain downright honesty and unintriguing integrity will be kicked out of doors."

He had been made a brigadier general of the Virginia militia, and he put his demands for strict enforcement of the neutrality law into direct action in the spring of 1794 by leading troops to the small port of Smithfield to halt French sympathizers still active there. They were operating the ship *Unicorn* as a privateer and had mounted a dozen cannon and other arms in a house that commanded the port. Reports were that the surrounding countryside was armed to the teeth and ready to resist any Federal attempt to seize the vessel.

General Marshall rode at the head of a cavalry unit, followed by light infantry and artillery, and supported by other small troop units dispatched by a revenue cutter from Norfolk. But the sight of his little army was enough to end resistance and no shots were fired. He took over the munitions and the ship and stopped Smithfield's defiance of the law of the United States.

Most of his pursuits were less military. As a lawyer managing the business transactions of wealthy men he was involved in a maze of often complicated legal routine, buying and selling land, drawing contracts and deeds, organizing companies. Among them was one of America's first fire insurance companies. He also had become an outstanding courtroom attorney, who during a period of half a dozen years, argued more than a hundred cases before Virginia's highest courts.

In the courtroom he preferred to let associates present the legal precedents, while he closed the cases with final arguments. He listened carefully to his adversaries and often informed himself about legal technicalities by taking knowledge from them. Unusually frank in court, he sometimes admitted his opponents were right and he had been wrong. A contemporary wrote that while Marshall could "hardly be regarded as a learned lawyer" he was a "common law lawyer in the best and noblest acceptation of that term."

His voice was hard and dry, deep with Southern accent, his words precise and carefully chosen. Tall, gaunt, bony thin, he was described by a friend of those years as having "joints loosely connected," so that his whole appearance seemed relaxed in "attitudes, gesture, sitting, standing or walking." His complexion was swarthy, his face expressed "great good humor," and his black eyes had "an irradiating spirit."

Marshall did the family marketing and frequently was seen with a market basket in one hand and a turkey or leg of meat in the other. In summer, when cherries were ripe, he liked to fill his hat with them and carry it in the crook of his arm, popping cherries into his mouth while, bare-headed, he sauntered about town. He enjoyed stopping to chat with people and exchanging news with travelers at the hotel or at Farmicola's tavern. He still loved the country and often rose at daybreak to ride out to a farm he had bought on the outskirts of Richmond. When he and Polly vacationed in Fauquier County at the old Marshall place at Oak Hill, he enjoyed riding in the woods, taking long walks in the hills, being alone in some quiet place to watch the sunset.

Every Saturday in good weather he and some thirty other companions gathered at the Richmond farm of an Episcopalian clergyman to hold an informal meeting of what became known as the Barbecue Club, to enjoy food, drink, general foolery and playing quoits. Socially, it was an exclusive group of Richmond's most prominent men, all close friends, who indulged in practical jokes, mock courts, and thorough relaxation.

Marshall spurned the small, polished brass quoits most players preferred and had his own set of big ones, rough and of heavy iron, that he had used for many years. Disputed shots sometimes were debated by the lawyers and judges present as if they were arguing a case in court. But when the debates grew too wordy, Marshall was likely to settle the issue by getting down on his hands and knees, plucking a blade of grass and measuring the distances the disputed quoits lay from the pin. From that decision, he would say, there was no appeal.

On a two-acre city square he had built what was then an imposing nine-room brick mansion, the house that was to be his Richmond home the rest of his life. At one side of the lot was a small white-painted frame building that was his law office. The house itself was square, simple, but with spacious rooms, and the neighborhood was Richmond's most fashionable. Polly's parents and three brothers-in-law, all firm Federalists like himself, had homes on adjoining squares.

The dining room, which also served as a library for his growing collection of books, was the scene of what became known as Marshall's "lawyers' dinners," gatherings of leading members of the bar that were a tradition he continued all his life. It soon became a mark of some success in Virginia, both socially and in the legal profession, to be among Marshall's few dozen invited guests. The dinners were much talked-about events, celebrated for elaborate foods and excellent wines as much as for the wit and brilliance of those who attended.

He and Polly had their sorrows. The death of a six-year-old daughter was followed within two summer months by the death of an infant son. Polly was so distracted she went to her mother's house, insisting she could never bear to return home. Marshall wrote to her in verse, turning to poetry as he often did to express his intimate feelings. He told her of his own sorrow over the deaths, but of the need he and their other children had for her. No one else ever saw it, but his poem brought Polly home.

Despite troubles and the hurt of political slander, the early 1790's were years of happiness and career success. He was a contented man, fairly certain he was doing what he would be doing the rest of his life. He had no other ambitions. There seemed to him nothing in the world that could tempt him to change the life he had. Richmond, Polly and his children were all the future he wanted.

8

J OHN MARSHALL was so determined not to leave Richmond that he refused in August, 1795, to become a member of George Washington's cabinet as Attorney General of the United States. Marshall was Washington's first choice to fill the vacancy left by the death of Will Bradford. In urging him to accept, the President pointed out that the salary was good and that Marshall could add to it by carrying on his private business as a lawyer in Philadelphia, where there were "prospects of lucrative practice."

But Marshall was earning three times as much in Richmond as the cabinet job would pay and had no ambition even for the highest of public offices if it meant leaving home. He wrote the President that while he felt "real pride and gratification" in being asked to join the cabinet, "the business I have undertaken to complete in Richmond forbids me to change my situation."

Marshall had by then become the President's chief political agent in Virginia, advising on Federal patronage and appointments. But with only a year of his second term left to go, Washington was so hated by many Americans, especially in his home state, that some demanded his impeachment. The new fury against Washington that Marshall said "seemed to rush through the Union with a rapidity and violence which set human reason and common sense at defiance" was over the treaty John Jay had made with England.

The United States, in trying to follow Washington's proclaimed policy of neutrality, was caught between warring France and England. The two nations, fighting for wartime supremacy at sea, were both seizing American ships and the goods they carried to keep them from supplying enemy ports. Sympathies at first were with the French. America had an ingrown hatred of the British left over from the Revolution and the British also were bolder than the French in plundering America's neutral shipping.

American protests accused the British of trying "to stifle the liberty of France and destroy our rising commerce and annihilate our growing navigation." When the British ignored all protests and high-handedly continued to seize American ships and cargoes and to force American sailors into service in the British navy, Marshall declared: "The man does not live who wishes for peace more than I do, but the outrages committed upon us are beyond human bearing."

But as the actual threat of a new war with England became real, Marshall sided with Washington and other Federalists who desperately tried to prevent it, believing such a war might destroy the nation. President Washington had borrowed John Jay, the first Chief Justice of the United States, from the Supreme Court and had sent him to London as a treaty maker. Jay had succeeded in making a new treaty that temporarily kept the peace, but at the price of giving the British just about everything they wanted and gaining nothing but time for the United States.

Anger and disgust swept the country. Washington and all Federalists including Marshall were accused of being pro-British. Protest meetings demanded Washington's removal from office and speakers charged that the government had prostrated itself before a British king "who had captured our vessels, enslaved our fellow-citizens, ruined our merchants, invaded our territory and trampled on our sovereignty." Jay was burned in effigy, Hamilton was stoned on the streets of Philadelphia, and people drank toasts to wish "a speedy death to General Washington." Washington himself complained that "the people have cried out against the Treaty as a mad dog."

Although friends warned Marshall that "the part . . . I would take would destroy me totally," he got himself elected to the Virginia legislature again to defend the treaty and President Washington. He believed that "even in times of violent spirit" a man "maintains his respectability by showing his strength, and is most safe when he encounters prejudice most fearlessly."

But he led a losing battle in Virginia's House of Delegates against Jefferson's Republicans, who made political capital of the public fury. Virginia's Federal senators had voted against ratifying the Jay treaty and Republicans who dominated the state legislature meant to pass a resolution praising them and putting Washington's home state on record as condemning his leadership of the country. They hoped to encourage such opposition in all the states that Washington would be forced to withdraw approval of the treaty and Congress would vote against appropriating money to carry out its terms.

Debate centered on the Republican charge that the treaty was unconstitutional. Republicans claimed the President had no right to make treaties and commercial agreements with other nations unless he had the approval of the entire Congress, including the House of Representatives, and not just the Senate alone. Marshall answered that the "words of the Constitution" itself gave the President his treaty-making power, with the consent of the Senate, and that it was also clearly based on the legitimate separation of powers granted the executive and legislative branches of government.

The only power the House of Representatives had over treaties, he declared, was in approving or rejecting appropriations to put them into effect. Since the President and Senate obviously had a right to make treaties, he accused his opponents of wasting the time of the Virginia legislature in unnecessary and pointless argument and made a motion to end the debate.

Infuriated Republicans voted him down and pushed through their original resolution by a two-to-one vote. Knowing he couldn't block it, Marshall tried to soften it with an amendment. He asked the legislature to declare that it was in no way questioning Washington's personal "wisdom" as the nation's leader. But Virginia's lawmakers refused to agree that Washington had shown any "wisdom."

Unable to defeat the move by the legislature, Marshall carried his battle to win support for the Jay treaty directly to the people of Richmond. He organized a public mass meeting and got several hundred Virginians to endorse a resolution that countered the one the legislature had passed. The "people's resolution" declared that the "peace, happiness and welfare" of the United States depended upon giving "full effect to the treaty lately negotiated with Great Britain." Actually the supporters were mostly Richmond Federalists, but Marshall at least produced an answer to the Republicans. Washington expressed his "very great satisfaction" over what he called "the *real* voice of the people."

While the controversy was boiling, Marshall made a trip to Philadelphia to argue his first and only case before the Supreme Court as a lawyer. The case of *Ware vs. Hylton* had attracted national attention as a test case that involved immense sums of money and interests in nearly all the states. It questioned laws passed by Virginia, and indirectly similar laws in other states, that during the Revolutionary War had cancelled the payment of debts Americans owed to British creditors.

British merchants and bankers trying to collect the long overdue debts had brought a number of suits in the new American courts on the grounds that treaty agreements between the United States and Britain pledged that "no legal impediments" would be placed in the way of debt collections. The Constitution provided that treaties were the supreme law of the land and the British argued that all judges in the states had to be bound by them, no matter what laws the states themselves had passed.

Marshall, as a lawyer, ironically had to defend principles that he had fought against all his public life. Personally and politically there were no causes he more strongly endorsed than the Constitution, the supremacy of Federal law, and the need for Americans to pay their rightful debts. But as an attorney, his personal views had no place in the court.

He had been hired to fight the claims of the British creditors and his role as a legal defender of the Virginia debtors was to use his best efforts against the very doctrines in which he most believed. Although he was battling against his own principles, he did so brilliantly. During the six days of argument before the Supreme Court, Marshall based his defense mainly on the claim that no debts existed because they had been wiped out by Virginia law before there was a national government or a treaty with Britain.

Marshall argued that Virginia had been an "independent nation" at the time it passed its law to confiscate British property as the legitimate act of an independent power at war with an attacking enemy. It was true that the treaty provided that "creditors" should not be prevented from collecting their debts, he admitted, but he said: "there cannot be a creditor where there is not a debt; and the British debts were extinguished by the act of confiscation."

The Supreme Court Justices ruled against him, probably to Marshall's private delight if not to his satisfaction as a lawyer. He lost the case but his presentation impressed other lawyers so much that some were still recommending it a quarter of a century later as a model for law students to study. Philadelphians made a temporary celebrity of him and, according to one account, he "was followed by crowds, looked upon and courted with every evidence of admiration and respect for the great powers of his mind."

Marshall himself much more modestly attributed his sudden popularity to the fact that a Federalist Virginian was such a "rare bird" in Federalist Philadelphia that people went out of their way to receive him "with a degree of kindness which I had not anticipated." In addition to spreading his fame as a lawyer, the Philadelphia visit gave Marshall a chance to become better acquainted with the Northerners who were the Congressional leaders of the Federalist party.

Such Congressional giants as Fisher Ames, George Cabot, Samuel Dexter and Theodore Sedgewick of Massachusetts, Peleg Wadsworth of Connecticut, and Rufus King of New York, sought him out, praised him, and saw to it that he was socially entertained. He became "particularly intimate with Ames," he wrote, and if he realized that his personal charm attracted them less than his possible political influence in the Southern states, Marshall nevertheless was "delighted with these gentlemen."

Meanwhile the United States, having escaped immediate war with England by means of the Jay treaty, found itself threatened with war by France because of the treaty. Revolutionary France was infuriated by the American pact with its British enemy, which it looked upon as a clear violation of America's self-proclaimed neutrality.

James Monroe, as American minister to France, had given free play to his Jeffersonian persuasions and was making public statements in Paris against the government he represented. President Washington felt Monroe was going behind his back to encourage the French to believe that it was only the Federalist administration and the President, not the American people, who were refusing to join France and fight England.

Back home in Richmond, Marshall soon received a confidential letter from President Washington. "In confidence I inform you," Washington wrote, "that it has become indispensably necessary to recall our minister at Paris and to send one in his place who will explain faithfully the views of this government and ascertain those of France. Nothing would be more pleasing to me than that you should be this organ, if it were only for a temporary absence of a few months."

In order to avoid any delay if Marshall felt he couldn't serve even on a temporary basis, Washington enclosed a letter to the man who was his second choice for the post, Charles Cotesworth Pinckney of South Carolina. The President asked Marshall to forward it immediately to Pinckney "if you decline the present offer" or to return it "if you accept it," and added, "Your own correct knowledge of the circumstances renders details unnecessary."

Marshall turned it down, just as he had Washington's previous offer of a place in the cabinet as Attorney General. He explained that it was impossible for him "in the present crisis of my affairs to leave the United States." Although he appreciated "the importance of that duty which you would confide to me," he hoped the President would understand his decision, and said, "I have forwarded your letter to Mr. Pinckney."

Washington previously had wanted to make Marshall head of his cabinet as Secretary of State, during one of the shake-ups which followed Jefferson's resignation. He also had wanted to put him on the joint British-American commission to settle claims under the Jay treaty. On that, Washington went so far as to write Virginia's state Attorney General Charles Lee to find out whether friends couldn't prevail upon Marshall to accept.

"I think it almost impossible," Lee answered the President. "Mr. Marshall is at the head of his profession in Virginia, enjoying every convenience and comfort, in the midst of his friends and the relations of his wife at Richmond . . . with a young and increasing family; and under a degree of necessity to continue his profession for the purpose of complying with contracts not yet performed."

The contracts were the ones Marshall and his syndicate had undertaken to buy up the Fairfax lands, the one major business transaction of his life, which he had hoped would build a future for himself and his sons. Instead, it was bringing financial troubles he never imagined when his wealthy friend Robert Morris had agreed to back the deal. Even more than his personal desire to remain in Richmond, that was the "crisis of my affairs" that had forced Marshall to turn down Washington's appeals to leave home and serve the government.

Robert Morris, who once had more money than nearly anybody else in America, also had bought more land than anybody else. Vast areas of the West could be had for a few dollars an acre and much of what was to become the new Federal District of Columbia could be bought cheaply, and with soaring faith in the coming expansion of the United States, Morris had put no limit on his speculations. Finally he went beyond even his enormous wealth. He discovered that foreign bankers were not so eager as he had hoped to lend money on American properties, and he faced bankruptcy that eventually was to put him in debtor's prison.

Morris had been able to raise enough in loans to finance the purchase of the Fairfax lands by the Marshall syndicate but on terms that became the heavy last straw that toppled his shaky financial pyramid. When it collapsed, the burden of making good on the Fairfax payments fell upon Marshall and his brother. Marshall struggled under the weight of it for years.

His immediate and desperate need for money was what finally forced him to undertake a diplomatic mission for the United States as a special envoy to France, for which the government would pay him some twenty thousand dollars. He also went because it was a mission in which he could serve his country and the principles in which he believed. But it was the need for funds that drove him to leave Richmond. The opportunity came, not from George Washington, but from John Adams, after he had been elected the new President.

By the time Washington declined to seek a third term in 1796 and prepared to retire to Mount Vernon, Jefferson was putting together his opposition party. Based on an alliance between Southern planters and the growing strength in the North of such groups as the Sons of Saint Tammany under ambitious young New York lawyer Aaron Burr, the Jeffersonian Republicans took in the French radical societies, discontented farmers and Western frontiersmen, and old opponents of the Constitution. Supporting states' rights and a minimum of national government, Jefferson and his followers were against almost everything Marshall's Federalists were for.

When Adams was elected President, Jefferson won enough votes to place second in the election and under the system then in effect became Vice-President although he was the leader of the opposition. President Adams found himself with a nation divided over the crisis in American relations with France. The Jeffersonians sympathized with the French, but many Federalists were on the point of demanding war against France.

The leaders of Revolutionary France, proud of their victorious armies in Europe and deeply angered by the Jay treaty and the recall of their warm friend, James Monroe, had in-

sultingly refused to receive Charles Cotesworth Pinckney as
the new American minister. The French had ordered Pinckney
out of the country under threat of arrest and had forced him
to seek refuge in Amsterdam.

Meanwhile the departing Monroe had been treated as a
French national hero. At an elaborate and affectionate leave-
taking ceremony in Paris, Monroe had attacked the Jay treaty
as "shameful," had charged that his removal as minister was
the work of American "aristocrats," and had given the French
an unauthorized pledge of the American people's "undying
friendship" for the cause of Revolution. In reply to Monroe,
the head of the French Directory, Paul François Nicholas,
comte de Barras, called upon Americans to rise against the
"tyrants" who headed their government and join their sister
republic in revolution. It was such an inflammatory speech it
brought the American Congress into special session.

President Adams told the Congress that Barras' speech was
"dangerous to our independence and union." He charged that
it was an open appeal "to separate the people of the United
States from the government, to persuade them that they had
different affections, principles and interests from those of their
fellow citizens . . . and thus to produce divisions fatal to our
peace." America, he declared, would repel such attempts to
degrade and humiliate the country with "miserable instruments
of foreign influence" that "cannot be disguised and will not
soon be forgotten." The French, he said, "have inflicted a
wound in the American breast."

But as angry as he was, Adams was not one to lose his
head in an emergency. He tried to quiet the temper of his
fellow Federalists who were demanding that Congress declare
war. Even with all the French raids on American shipping,
the formal insults to the government, and the attempt to divide
the people, the President said, "I shall institute a fresh attempt
at negotiation . . ."

Adams proposed an extraordinary mission to France of three special envoys and the Congress agreed. One was to be Pinckney, and the second, former Congressman Elbridge Gerry of Massachusetts, a patriot hero of the Revolution whom the President still considered an old and trusted friend even though Gerry had become a Jeffersonian. Since Adams knew that Marshall had been Washington's first choice to replace Monroe as minister to France, he called upon Marshall to become the third special envoy.

Marshall felt that this time he could not refuse. With Robert Morris heading into bankruptcy and the promise of government pay for the mission, plus the nation's urgent need for his services, he finally agreed to leave Richmond, although with the hope that he wouldn't be away for long.

He thus began what was to become the historic adventure in diplomatic intrigue known as the *XYZ Affair,* with a real-life plot of mysterious happenings that might have been taken from the imaginative fiction of a suspense thriller. Before the mission was half-over, Marshall would write, "Oh, God, how much time and how much happiness I have thrown away!" And never again would he return to the relatively calm and private life of a merely successful Virginia attorney at law.

9

J OHN MARSHALL, Minister Plenipotentiary and Envoy Extraordinary from the United States of America to the Republic of France, rode horseback to Mount Vernon late in June, 1797, for a long talk with George Washington, and then sailed up the bay from Baltimore for three weeks of conferences and instructions at the capital in Philadelphia.

But he hadn't gone beyond the Virginia border before he stopped to write Polly that "I cannot help feeling a pang when I reflect that every step I take carries me further and further from what is to me most valuable in this world." He hoped the whole mission would be done with speedily so that "I shall see you again to be the two happiest persons on earth," and he wrote: "Farewell—I was never peremptory but I must now give you one positive order. It is to be happy."

He had a private dinner with President Adams as soon as he arrived in Philadelphia and received detailed instructions from Secretary of State Timothy Pickering. Alexander Hamilton came from New York to talk to him, and to predict rightly that the French Republic was on the verge of dictatorship.

Finally, late in July, 1797, he sailed down the Delaware

Bay aboard the brig *Grace,* to begin the ocean crossing that
would take him to meet Pinckney in Holland, with the hope
that Gerry would soon join them there. Marshall hurried to
his cabin to write a last-minute note to Polly as "the land is
just escaping from my view and the pilot is about to leave
us." His cabin was neat and clean, he wrote, his berth com-
modious, he had enough fresh sheets, had brought along
"more books than I can read," and "we have for the voyage
the greatest plenty of salt provisions, live stock and poultry."
But he entreated Polly to write him often. "Some of your
letters may miscarry but some will reach me. . . . Your happiness will ever be the first prayer."

The voyage to Europe took seven weeks and the *Grace*
escaped the French sea rovers that everywhere were interfering with American shipping, but British warships halted
the brig three times. When boarding parties were informed
that Marshall was a passenger as Envoy Extraordinary of
the United States, the *Grace* courteously was allowed to pro-
ceed. Closer to land, a British captain also permitted Marshall's
ship to pass through the blockade of the Dutch harbor, and
he at last arrived at The Hague on September 6, 1797.
Pinckney, ousted from France as the American minister, was
waiting to greet him, and the two developed an immediate
liking for each other.

But there was also bad news. In Paris only days before,
an army *coup d'état* had overthrown the more moderate ele-
ments of government and had made Barras virtual dictator
of the Directory, taking strength from the rising power of
General Napoleon Bonaparte. Conservatives had been forced
out, majority members of the legislature arrested, the press
put under a gag of censorship, and those who had seized
control were not likely to favor any new agreement to settle
difficulties with the United States.

There was no letters from Polly awaiting Marshall in Holland, and he received none for weeks after he eventually reached Paris. The lack of news from home worried him almost as much as the diplomatic ordeal. He wrote her that "my mind clings so much to Richmond," and told her he was so uneasy and troubled he regretted "having ever consented to cross the Atlantic."

He and Pinckney, after waiting a while for Gerry to join them in Holland, finally decided to go on to Paris. They reached the French capital the end of September and Gerry soon arrived there. Marshall meanwhile did a bit of sightseeing, visiting the theaters and the glittering Paris opera house, and wrote Polly, "All you can conceive and a great deal more than you can conceive in the line of amusement is to be found in this gay metropolis but I suspect it would not be easy to find a friend."

Certainly the American envoys found no friend in the person of the new French Minister of Foreign Affairs, the brilliant and deceitful Charles Maurice de Talleyrand. Born to the high nobility and turned radical, he had been Bishop of Autun before he was excommunicated for his revolutionary activities and was forced to flee to exile in the United States, where he spent two years in poverty and learned to hate almost everything American. Brought back to France and to favor by the Directory and made Foreign Minister, Talleyrand had firmly hitched himself and his future to Napoleon, around whom he would spin the spiderwebs of intrigue that were to win him lasting notoriety as a mastermind of both diplomacy and betrayal.

For Marshall, Pinckney, and Gerry, he plotted a labyrinth of delays and frustrations to stall any agreement, divide the mission, and produce a failure that he hoped would lead to the overthrow of the American Federalist government. He meant to force the weak and as yet almost defenseless United States to bow to the dictates of France while paying a great tribute in money to avoid being destroyed by war. In the process, Talleyrand also hoped to line his own pockets and those of his friends with rich bribes.

Any nation that failed to stand with France against Britain was to Talleyrand an enemy, not a neutral, and any agreement would be on the terms he demanded for France and only after the United States filled the needy treasury of French Revolution with gold. But Talleyrand was too much the clever schemer to present such demands himself or in the name of the French government. Marshall and the envoys he led were to hear of such things only in whispers from Talleyrand's very secret agents.

The first meeting between Talleyrand and the envoys was the last they were to have with him for two months. In answer to their request to present their credentials, he received them informally at his home, intimating that their errand was hardly worth his formal attention. He appeared almost disdainfully unimpressed by the three men he saw before him.

Gerry, the New Englander, was a small, erect, fastidiously dressed little sparrow of a man, with a solemn face, long nose and enormous wig. Talleyrand had met him before in Boston, knew that with his Jeffersonian faith Gerry would be more sympathetic toward France than the others, and meant to use him as the cat's-paw of his plot to divide the loyalties of the group.

Pinckney, the South Carolinian, was a portly, hearty, blunt military man, transparently honest and outspoken, worldly and pleasure-loving, and without subtlety. Talleyrand had dealt with him before, when France had refused to accept him as minister in Monroe's place, and for Pinckney he had nothing but plain contempt.

Marshall was ten years younger than the others, the same age as Talleyrand, forty-two. Tall, ungainly, pleasant-faced, awkward in social grace, lacking in style of dress, he was un-known to Talleyrand except by reputation. Because of that, Talleyrand treated him more warily than the others.

Talleyrand must have seemed to Marshall, as to most people who met him, one of the physically ugliest men he had ever seen. Scarecrow thin, pallid-faced, with puffy and slumberous eyes and hollow cheeks, halting in speech and slow-moving, he walked with a limp, dragging the twisted foot that had kept him from a military career as a youth and turned him to the priesthood instead. His voice was a purr that seldom brought his words to any direct point without first toying with them.

He said that he was a very busy man who had no time to discuss anything with them at the moment. Implying that the United States was only a third-rate power and that France had many more vital interests that demanded his attention, he did offer to give them "cards of hospitality" so they would not be harassed by police. Before dismissing them, he told them they would be informed of "what steps are to follow."

Talleyrand meant to wear thin their patience and their nerves by refusing to admit them to his presence again until they had bought the right to another audience and were ready to bargain on the terms France demanded. France, supported by its victorious armies, was already adopting the methods of dictatorship Napoleon soon would fully enforce. Talleyrand's Foreign Office simply informed the helpless countries within reach of French military power that if they hoped to enjoy peace instead of destruction they had to pay for it with subsidies and loans, as well as with pledges of friendship and co-operation.

Loot had been extorted for the French treasury, as well as bribes for the members of the Directory, from Portugal, the Netherlands and the German city-states, the richest trading areas of the Continent. Talleyrand saw no reason why the

United States should be treated differently, and to bring Marshall and the other envoys around to that point of view he arranged a softening-up process. While he kept them waiting, he tried to impress and alarm them with the dangers America would suffer if they failed to offer France the proper tribute.

As a stage-setting preliminary, Talleyrand had a procession of Americans who were living in Paris call on the envoys. They were businessmen, merchants and shipowners and they had sorrowful tales to tell of the terrible depredations being committed against American ships and crews by the French sea raiders. Sailors were being mistreated, ships were being seized, valuable cargoes were lost, and the visitors pleaded with their envoys to make whatever deal they could to put an end to the increasing piracy of French privateers.

Then began the parade of Talleyrand's secret agents, X, Y, and Z, whose mysterious comings and goings were detailed in the dispatches Marshall sent the State Department, largely based on the notes he kept in his journal. Agent X was a Swiss financier named Hottenguer, carefully selected by Talleyrand because he had spent some time in America and also had been among the Amsterdam bankers who helped raise European loans for the Fairfax land purchase. Marshall had never met him and probably had never heard of him before, but Pinckney had become acquainted with Hottenguer in Holland.

After much small-talk, Hottenguer whispered Pinckney into the next room, away from Marshall and Gerry, and with great caution informed him that he had a message from Talleyrand. The Foreign Minister, according to his agent, really wanted to be friendly toward America, but certain members of the French Directory were still enraged over the speech President Adams had made to Congress in reply to what Barras had said when Monroe was recalled. Talleyrand, he went on, would not even risk sitting down to talk to the envoys again unless the feelings of Directory members could be soothed.

Hottenguer suggested that the way to soothe their feelings was with money, "put at the disposal of Talleyrand," to be spread to the pockets of the irate members of the Directory. Once that was done, then perhaps Talleyrand could arrange another meeting with the envoys, where they would be permitted to apologize in the name of the United States for President Adams' "insulting" remarks about Barras.

When Pinckney wanted to know how much of a bribe Talleyrand had in mind, Hottenguer said that the "small amount" of one quarter of a million dollars might do for a start. After that, the United States would be required to pay France a subsidy in the form of loans for many millions of dollars more, and also guarantee to pay off all claims for debts that France owed to American citizens, as well as claims for damage done to commerce by French privateers. But before those terms would be considered, the bribe had to be paid or Talleyrand would not talk to the envoys at all.

Marshall, when he learned the details of what had been whispered to Pinckney, was "decidedly of the opinion that such a proposition could not be made by a nation from whom any treaty short of the absolute surrender of the independence of the United States was to be expected." He wrote that if the mission was to have any chance of reaching an agreement with France, it would be wrong "to give any countenance whatever" to the message brought by Hottenguer because "it would induce France to demand from us terms to which it is impossible for us to accede."

He thought they ought to take no notice of Hottenguer and should "break off this indirect mode of procedure" and file a protest on behalf of "our countrymen" against the "most unusual and contemptuous" manner in which France had tried to deal with them. Pinckney agreed with him, but Gerry argued that such a step would rupture all relations and might "bring war between the two nations." Marshall and Pinckney, to keep the mission from breaking up, finally gave in to Gerry's plea that they should at least find out whether there was any way to reason with Talleyrand.

When they tried to get Hottenguer to put the proposition in writing, he said he had been merely making suggestions that had come to him, not directly from Talleyrand but "through another gentleman in whom Talleyrand has great confidence." That gentleman was Secret Agent Y, a Mr. Bellamy, who was described to them as "a Genevan now residing in Hamburg but in Paris on a visit." Hottenguer brought Bellamy to Marshall's candlelit room the next evening and the envoys heard him out.

Bellamy explained that he had been a visitor to America and that the generous way he had been treated there had "touched his heart," so he wanted to "repay these kindnesses." The Directory was so angered by President Adams' speech that it refused to allow Talleyrand "to have any communication" with the envoys, he said, so he had been sent to deal with them in secret and to promise that if they agreed to Talleyrand's terms some way might be found to get the Foreign Minister to receive them. But Bellamy also explained that he was "clothed with no authority," was not speaking for the government, and was acting only as "Talleyrand's friend" in an attempt to help the envoys save themselves and their country.

Bellamy's "advice" was a repetition of the previous demands. He told them, "You must pay money—a great deal of money." When the two-hour talk ended, Marshall was indignant and so was Pinckney. Gerry thought the propositions should be considered, but Marshall declared "that I would not consent . . . that the subject was already considered and that so far as my voice would go I would not permit it to be supposed longer that we could deliberate on such propositions as were made to us."

From then on, Marshall had a constant tug-of-war with Gerry, trying to keep him in line and hold the mission together, while the Jeffersonian Gerry went off on his own to secret meetings with Talleyrand's various agents, convinced that he personally knew what was best for America. Gerry, following the devious paths down which he was led, even managed to meet with Talleyrand himself a few times in private. Once, Gerry reported, Talleyrand actually wrote out his terms to show them to him, and then dramatically burned the paper on which they were written.

Agent Z now came upon the scene, a man named Hauteval who had made his fortune in the West Indies, and who hinted at the trade advantages America might acquire if the raids on shipping were halted and the United States gained French protection by winning back its friendship. But he had nothing new to offer that the Americans could accept.

Meanwhile Napoleon's military victories, which permitted him to impose upon Austria peace on his own terms, strengthened Talleyrand's hand. Talleyrand's agents began warning that France would next throw its full might against England, that the British would be doomed, and that if the United States hoped to escape the same fate then its envoys had better quickly soothe the Directory with the necessary bags of gold. Pinckney lost his temper at that and roared, "No, not a sixpence!"

But by the end of the year France was making an immense show of preparations for a supposed invasion of England and Talleyrand's agents warned Marshall that the last defense between the United States and an all-powerful France was about to crumble. Bellamy voiced the direct threat that not only would America be next if the envoys failed to come to terms, but that it would be a divided nation, unable to resist.

All the "diplomatic skill of France and the means she possesses in your country," Marshall quoted Bellamy as saying, "are sufficient to enable her, with the French Party in America, to throw the blame which will attend the rupture of negotiations on the Federalists . . . and you may assure yourselves that this will be done."

It was not a threat Marshall took lightly. As he saw the military preparations against England, he wrote George Washington, "It is perhaps justly believed that on this issue is staked the independence of Europe and America." Yet he shrewdly guessed that as long as the British held dominion over the seas the French would not rush into any real attempt to strike England across the Channel, and that the preparations were mostly a bluff designed as a threatening show of strength.

With other foreign diplomats, Marshall watched Paris give a wild hero's welcome to the conquering Napoleon, when he appeared in the city fresh from his military triumphs early in December. Marshall was somewhat surprised by Napoleon's small stature, and noted that in contrast to the glitter of other uniforms the general wore a strikingly simple gray riding coat. He also was much aware of the fact that Talleyrand stood at Napoleon's side.

Having failed so far with his other agents, Talleyrand brought two more into the plot. One, in the tradition of foreign intrigue, was a charming, not so young, but still gracious, witty and attractive lady, Madame de Vilette, who tried to use the softer wiles of diplomacy by hinting prettily that the envoys would do well to give in to the French. Another had been a law client of Marshall's in a long-pending suit in America, the dashing and adventurous man of letters, Pierre Augustin Caron de Beaumarchais, author of *The Barber of Seville* and *The Marriage of Figaro*.

As a secret agent for the monarchy long before the Revolution in France, Beaumarchais had worked in America to furnish several million dollars worth of war supplies from France during the American Revolution. The United States was years in settling his claims, some of which finally were paid to his heirs by an act of Congress after his death. Meanwhile he had hired Marshall as his Virginia attorney to press one of the many suits he filed in American courts. Beaumarchais gave a dinner in Paris for Marshall and his fellow envoys and they exchanged the courtesy and gave a dinner for him.

Beaumarchais then dropped out of the picture for a time, but Talleyrand's "confidential friend" Bellamy reappeared with a new suggestion to make. It should be simple enough, Bellamy whispered to Marshall, for the American government to put pressure on its courts to decide the pending law suit in Beaumarchais' favor. If Beaumarchais won the case, he would be willing to turn over $250,000 of the award so the Americans could bribe Talleyrand with it, and the whole deal could be pulled off without any loss of money by the United States.

Marshall's answer was that American courts didn't work that way. He said he would not only have no part in such a scheme, but he would no longer act as a lawyer for Beaumarchais and "would not by my voice establish any argument in his favor, but... would positively oppose any admission of the claim."

But the pressures were beginning to wear on the envoys and Gerry was in almost constant dispute with Pinckney and Marshall. Gerry thought they were provoking war by failing to give in to the French, and they suspected him of going behind their backs to deal with the French. Marshall more than once lost his temper with Gerry.

The negotiations, never officially started, reached a complete standstill. Entirely on his own in the fateful decisions he had to make, since communication with the far-off American government was too slow for instructions, Marshall drafted a letter to Talleyrand which would state the American position of neutrality. It was a long statement, but clear, logical and strongly worded, expressing the desire of the United States to treat France as it had England under the Jay treaty, by extending equal friendship to both warring lands while staying at peace with the world. With much persuasion, he and Pinckney got Gerry to join them in signing it.

Talleyrand let it be known that he was too busy with important matters to read it, and turned it over to a clerk to be filed and forgotten. But after it had been lying unread in his office for a month, while Marshall and Pinckney showed no signs of weakening, Talleyrand finally condescended to let all three envoys visit him together, only to hear from him the same demands his secret agents already had made.

When he still failed to shake them, Talleyrand issued a statement of his own, designed for publication in America, where he hoped it would arouse public rage against the envoys. He singled out Marshall and Pinckney as being apart from Gerry, who as a Jeffersonian Republican of the French Party represented the "real desire" of the American people to reach a friendly agreement with France. President Adams, he implied, had tried to thwart the will of the people by sending Marshall and Pinckney as envoys, since they were "persons whose opinions and connections are too well known to hope from them dispositions sincerely conciliatory." He suggested that Marshall and Pinckney should go back to America and leave Gerry in Paris to negotiate a treaty.

Marshall answered that they were not authorized to entrust their mission to any one member and Gerry as well as Pinckney joined him in signing the letter. But Gerry decided to remain for a time in Paris when Marshall and Pinckney packed up to go home. Talleyrand delayed issuing Marshall's passport as a last small gesture of contempt, but it finally came through. Without bidding good-by to Gerry, who accomplished nothing by staying, Marshall saw Pinckney off to rejoin the Pinckney family in Holland, and himself went to Bordeaux.

There, on April 24, 1798, he set sail for the United States aboard the ship *Alexander Hamilton.* He had done what he felt the honor and independence of his country required in resisting the French demands for bribery and tribute. But his mission to obtain a treaty had failed and Marshall felt he had wasted a year of his life. He didn't know that in his absence his dispatches to America had made him a national hero.

10

J OHN MARSHALL'S ship reached New York in mid-June, 1798,
after fifty-two days at sea where he had been completely
cut off from all news of the world. Rested and refreshed by
the voyage, he was still bitter over the ordeal he had gone
through in Paris. He was to write of it: "History will scarcely
furnish the example of a nation, not absolutely degraded,
which has experienced from a foreign power such open
contumely and undisguised insult."

He didn't know, when he arrived in New York, that most
of his country agreed with him. His dispatches had reached
President Adams when things were going badly for the Federalists and for the President in his efforts to arouse the public
to prepare for possible war with France. Jefferson and his
pro-French Republicans, hotly opposing the preparedness
measures, were making political headway almost everywhere,
even in normally Federalist New England.

Delayed almost five months in transit, Marshall's early dispatches to the State Department finally reached President
Adams on his first anniversary in office, March 4, 1798. As
Adams read of the French insults and demands for bribes,
loans and apologies, he knew he had in his hands information

that might turn the political tide back to the Federalists. He spent two weeks preparing a restrained message to Congress that, without revealing any details, admitted that the mission had failed but declared that it was because the French were not willing to deal with Marshall and the other envoys "on terms compatible with the safety, the honor, or the essential interests of the nation." Adams called upon Congress to build up the Army and Navy and to arm merchant ships to defend the nation against France.

Jefferson called the President's message "almost insane," suspected it was a Federalist trick to hide the truth of what had really happened in the Paris negotiations, and had his leaders in Congress put through a resolution demanding that President Adams make public the dispatches. By "exposing the truth to public view," the Republicans hoped to prove the envoys actually had rebuffed friendly overtures for peace by the French government.

Adams hesitated just long enough to fan the Republican suspicions and then sent the papers to Congress. He made one slight change in Marshall's dispatches that was a master stroke of propaganda. Adams eliminated the names of Talleyrand's secret agents Hottenguer, Bellamy and Hauteval "to protect their diplomatic identity" and designated them only as X, Y, and Z.

Spread before the American people and the stunned and unhappy Jeffersonians, the sinister plotting of the alphabetical French secret agents became the most avidly read and talked about foreign intrigue story of the age, more exciting than any fictional tale because it was true. Marshall was the obvious hero of the honorable men who had stood against the corrupt officials of a corrupt foreign government and refused to submit to their demands for bribery and tribute.

The "foul conspiracy" against the United States whipped Americans into a frenzy of national hysteria against the

French and also against Jefferson's Republicans who favored the French. Preachers took to their pulpits to exhort congregations to support Federalism and preparedness, newspapers printed raging editorials, public meetings denounced France and French-loving Republicans. Those who not long before had worn French Liberty Caps donned the black cockades of the American Revolution. On the streets, in taverns and in theaters, the flag was waved and patriotic songs were sung.

It was the first real surge of national patriotism, of conscious allegiance to a Federal government, and it brought the country at least a temporary sense of unity as a people. But Marshall knew nothing of what had happened while he was away. His arrival in New York was unannounced and there were no hero-worshiping crowds to greet him. He hurried toward Philadelphia to report in person to the President. As he neared the city, news of his arrival spread ahead of him, and a welcoming party rode out to the suburbs to meet him on the road and to escort him into Philadelphia in triumph. He was amazed.

Federalist newspapers exaggerated the reception into "fleets of carriages and armies of horsemen" and reported that he was welcomed home with a demonstration "never before given any other American." But even Vice-President Jefferson, who had the least reason of anybody to be happy over the event, was impressed. Jefferson had stayed in Philadelphia to witness Marshall's arrival, and he wrote an account of it to Madison:

"Marshall was received here with the utmost éclat. The Secretary of State & many carriages, with all the city cavalry, went to Frankfort to meet him, and on his arrival here in the evening, the bells rung until late in the night & immense crowds were collected to see & make part of the show, which was circuitously paraded through the streets before he was set down at the city tavern."

The procession of important visitors who came to call on Marshall at his room in O'Eller's Hotel gave him little rest.

Among them was Jefferson himself, who called twice and found Marshall out both times, busy making reports to President Adams and Secretary of State Pickering. Jefferson left a card, expressing his regret at being "so unlucky" as not to find Marshall there, but by a slip of the pen wrote "lucky" and then corrected it by inserting "un" above the line. Long afterwards historians made much of the error, as a psychological slip that probably revealed Jefferson's true feelings toward Marshall.

As the hero of the hour Marshall was given a public dinner by the members of Congress, which was attended by the President's cabinet, the Justices of the Supreme Court, top-ranking officers of the Army, two Episcopal bishops, and "all of Philadelphia's distinguished personages." Outside, a cheering crowd turned to singing what was fast becoming the first national anthem: "Hail, Columbia! happy land!"

Inside the tavern where the feast was held, the distinguished guests drank liberally of Federalist wine and offered seventeen toasts to everything from the President, the People, and the Army, to the Constitution and the American Eagle. One of the toasts that soon echoed through the country translated Pinckney's cry of "No, not a sixpence!" into the slogan, "Millions for defense but not a cent for tribute!" The final toast was to Marshall: "The man whom his country delights to honor!"

President Adams also was prepared to tender him an honor, by appointing him to the place on the Supreme Court made vacant by the death of Justice James Wilson. But Marshall promptly and politely declined. All he wanted was to get away from the Federalist pageantry in Philadelphia as fast as he could. He felt he had earned his fee the hard way as Envoy Extraordinary, and while he was flattered to discover himself a hero, he did not relish the role or the public hysteria which had cast him for it.

Even more compelling were his personal anxieties. He had

just learned that months before, while he had been worrying in Paris over not hearing from her, Polly had given birth to a son, a boy he had never seen, named John for him. He also received the tragic news that Polly's father, Jacquelin Ambler, had died suddenly and that the shock had left Polly in a state of nervous collapse.

According to her sister Eliza, Polly had fallen "into a deep melancholy from which no one could relieve her." She had lost interest in everything in life, even the baby, who had been left in the care of servants at their Richmond home while Polly was taken to Winchester in Northern Virginia to stay with relatives.

With two thousand dollars in the belt strapped around his waist, money paid to him on account by the State Department, Marshall rode to Winchester. He found Polly had recovered somewhat in the time it took the news of her illness to reach him, and their reunion greatly brightened her spirits. But he spent nearly a month with her in Winchester, taking her for long horseback rides, seeing that she was surrounded with cheerful friends, and going with her to the nearby mineral springs where the baths were considered a health restorative.

Her nerves were still too unsettled to stand the strain and summer heat of Richmond, so she remained in Winchester while he went on home alone to take care of the urgent legal and business matters that had been so long neglected. But he soon wrote her he "scarcely had time to look into any business yet, there are so many persons calling every hour to see me."

Getting acquainted again with his three-year-old daughter Mary, he found her "the most fascinating little creature I ever beheld . . . the most coquetish little prude and the most prudish little coquet I ever saw." Like any proud father, he boasted in a letter to Polly that baby John "appeared to know me as soon as he saw me." He would be a happy man, he wrote, if he could ony know that Polly's health was restored and that she would return to him in October "quite yourself."

Marshall never did get back to his law business. He was caught up in a new political furor that swept the United States. While he was trying to untangle his business affairs in Richmond, his Federalist party all but committed political suicide. The temporary wave of public opinion that had lifted the Federalists to new popularity crashed down upon them when they tried to enforce their hold on the national government by practically making it a Federal crime to be a Republican.

The war scare and outraged feelings against France led the more hotheaded Federalists to push stern laws through Congress that were aimed at stamping out subversive activities. The Alien and Sedition Laws were intended to rid the country of foreigners accused of working against the United States, to silence French sympathizers, and to halt abusive newspaper attacks against the President and other leaders of the government.

But the Federalist extremists also saw the chance finally to crush Jefferson's rising Republican party. Goaded by their fears of losing power and by the temporary popularity that went to their heads, and ignoring the warnings of moderate Federalists that the people would never accept oppression in the name of the law, the party's leaders in Congress drove the measures through. They launched America's first political "witch hunt," designed to brand anyone who dared to disagree with their views as a dangerous radical enemy of the nation.

The Alien Acts drastically tightened naturalization and citizenship requirements and threatened foreigners with being arrested, imprisoned or banished at the will of the President, without any right of trial or appeal. President Adams actually made little attempt to enforce the Alien Acts, but Federalist threats and blustering terrorized some foreigners, including some agents of the French government, into fleeing from the United States, and drove others into hiding.

More drastic were the Sedition Acts, which struck directly at the rights of American citizens by making opposition to the government a crime. Any American who dared to criticize the President or the Congress by speaking or writing about them in such a way as "to bring them . . . into contempt or disrepute or to excite against them . . . the hatred of the good people of the United States" could be fined or thrown into jail.

The Federalists thought they had found a way to silence Republican newspapers and speakers on pain of imprisonment. As a warning, they began rounding up some of their more outspoken opponents, and with the help of Federalist judges, railroading them into jail. Again, the threat was greater than the actual enforcement, but some twenty-five arrests were made and there were ten convictions, mostly of Republican editors.

But America's citizens were not about to be told that they could no longer exercise their freedom of speech. Contempt for politicians, far from being a crime, was a well-established American custom, and the rage of the people rose with nothing but contempt for the Federalists. Instead of being silenced, Republican newspapers became more violently defiant than ever in attacks against the government. Speakers harangued mass meetings, states passed resolutions of protest, and jailed Republicans were hailed as martyrs to the cause of independence and the rights of free men.

The blundering Federalist "witch hunters" were destroying their own party, and Jefferson's Republicans had never enjoyed such overwhelming public backing. George Washington, drawn out of retirement by the French war scare, had accepted command of the new Army and he now feared that the government in which he believed was falling apart. In his own Virginia the Federalists were in such disrepute he became convinced that only Marshall could win the people's confidence. He summoned Marshall to Mount Vernon to try to enlist him as a candidate for Congress from the Richmond district.

He knew Marshall would be reluctant, so he sent his lawyer nephew, Bushrod Washington, long a friend of Marshall's, to press the urgency of the trip, and the two traveled together to Mount Vernon. On the way, after an overnight stop at an inn, they picked up somebody else's saddlebags instead of their own and didn't discover the mistake until after they rode all day through a downpour of rain that drenched them to the skin. When Marshall arrived at Mount Vernon and went to change his things, he found only the worn and dirty pants of some wagoner in the bag, and had to wear those to go down to dinner with Washington. His appearance brought a roar of laughter from his host, but Washington and Marshall soon were not smiling.

They liked each other too well to become angry, but they argued through most of the next four days as Washington tried to convince Marshall he should run for Congress and Marshall stubbornly, if respectfully, refused. Washington told him it was "his duty." Marshall answered that he had already done his duty by wasting a year of his life going to Paris, that his law practice had been neglected, that he was under the heavy burden of the Fairfax estate debts, that his wife was ill, that he had just turned down appointment to the Supreme Court because he couldn't afford to leave Richmond again.

But Washington was a man Marshall admired more than any other, and he argued that nobody had a right to put private affairs before his country's need. He told Marshall that he personally needed his voice in Congress, that the Federalists needed him, Virginia needed him, and he pointed out that he himself had given up the comforts of retirement to serve his country again. Marshall at last unhappily gave in. As he put it, "My resolution yielded to this representation." He wrote Secretary of State Pickering that he had "as punishment for some unknown sins, consented to be named a candidate for the ensuing election to Congress."

The election contest was the bitterest political battle Marshall had gone through. He took a firm stand against the Alien and Sedition Laws and was caught in a cross-fire between Republicans who denounced him as an insincere hypocrite and intemperate Federalists who accused him of turning against his own party.

Marshall declared his support for administration policies toward France and toward agents and sympathizers of France who were working within the United States, but with equal firmness made it clear he was "certainly no advocate" of "useless and repressive laws that should never have been enacted." They were, he said, "calculated to create unnecessary discontents and jealousies . . . at a time when our very existence as a nation may depend upon our union." He said that if he had been in Congress when they were passed, he would have voted against them, and he promised that if elected he would vote against their renewal and vote for their repeal.

President Adams meanwhile had caused a new rupture in Federalist ranks. With the party's war hawks supporting him because they believed he was all for going to war against France, and with his own political future depending upon it, Adams bravely and wisely decided to seek peace.

American merchant ships were warring unofficially with French vessels at sea and the nation was ready to send its new fourteen-ship Navy into the fray. But Napoleon had taken control in France and, faced for the time with enough troubles of his own in Europe, had let it be known that France would welcome another peace mission and would make an honest attempt to work out a treaty with the United States.

When Adams agreed to send new envoys many Federalists turned against him, and when Marshall supported the peace move some charged that he had betrayed his own stand in Paris and had gone over to the side of Jefferson and the Republicans. Marshall answered that by pointing out that the whole purpose of his own mission had been to avoid war with France.

As election day neared, Marshall doubted that he would win. Then Virginia's Republicans played into his hands by claiming that the great old patriot, Patrick Henry, had joined them in the fight to keep Marshall from going to Congress. With a flash of his old fire, Henry declared that not a word of it was true. He would, he said, rather vote for Marshall than any other man in Virginia, and he intimated that no real patriot could do less. "Tell Marshall I love him," he wrote, "because he felt and acted as a republican, as an American."

Marshal won the election by 108 votes. Polly went with him when he took his seat in the House of Representatives in December, 1799, for the start of the Sixth Congress of the United States. They enjoyed making the social rounds of Philadelphia together, which included a formal visit to the Schuylkill River home of Vice-President Jefferson, as well as a call on President and Mrs. Adams.

But two weeks after the session of Congress began, passengers on a stagecoach traveling through Philadelphia brought the shocking rumor that George Washington had died. Marshall rose in the House, tears on his face, to inform Congress that "information has just been received that our illustrious fellow-citizen . . . the late President of the United States, is no more." He moved for an adjournment and the next day, when the news had been confirmed, he announced to Congress that "The Hero, the Sage, and the Patriot of America—the man on whom in times of danger every eye was turned and all hopes were placed—lives now only in his great actions, and in the hearts of an affectionate and afflicted people." Marshall then read the resolutions of mourning, written by General

Henry Lee, that immortally described Washington as "first in war, first in peace, and first in the hearts of his countrymen."

As a Congressman, although he voted with the Federalists on routine matters, Marshall became increasingly independent of the party on issues he personally opposed. He kept his pledge to vote for repeal of the Sedition Act and by standing against his own party broke a tie vote and carried repeal through the House, although the Senate later delayed final action until the next Congress. He also angered others in his party by speaking and voting against a Federalist measure to change election procedures in a way that might be used to deny votes to Republicans. Despite being only a freshman member of the House, Marshall all but took control of several important committees, was chosen to head Congressional delegations to call on President Adams, and also distinguished himself in debate.

In one floor battle, Marshall presented such a full and convincing argument that Republican leader Albert Gallatin tossed away the notes he had been making for a reply. When fellow Republicans urged Gallatin to answer Marshall's argument, he told them: "Answer it yourselves. For my part, I think it unanswerable."

As it became almost certain that Jefferson would win the next election in 1800, quarrels within the Federalist party grew and President Adams finally lost his temper. All through his administration his party enemy, Alexander Hamilton, had been trying to undermine him politically. When Adams discovered that Hamilton was interfering with his cabinet, even to the point of writing reports that cabinet members presented as their own, Adams fired his two principal advisers, Secretary of War James McHenry and Secretary of State Timothy Pickering.

Without consulting Marshall, President Adams appointed him Secretary of War, but Marshall refused to accept. A few days later, this time asking him in advance, Adams requested him to become Secretary of State. Marshall thought it over for two weeks.

He still wanted to be in Richmond. Even more than when George Washington had forced him to accept the term in Congress, he wanted to be home with his wife and family, practicing the profession of law. The position of Secretary of State paid so little he felt that with the financial burdens he had he simply couldn't afford it. He was being asked to take command of a cabinet that had been wrecked, for an administration that was shattered, backed by a party that was divided and all but destroyed.

But whatever its faults and its quarrels might be, it was a party that had established the strong national government in which he believed and in an election year the staggered administration needed men of some reputation in the cabinet. So Marshall finally agreed to serve as Secretary of State, expecting that it probably wouldn't be for long, since it was almost certain that Adams would be out of office after the election. Whatever happened, when that was over, Marshall was determined to quit public life forever and go back to Richmond to stay.

→≫ CHAPTER ≪←

11

J OHN MARSHALL took up his duties as Secretary of State in
the summer of 1800 in a new capital, the fever-ridden,
steaming hot, dust-clouded, mosquito-infected, pioneer town of
frame houses and uncompleted government buildings erected
on the mud flats of a swamp that was the new Federal city of
Washington. He was among the first top government officials
to arrive; most others stayed away as long as they had any
excuse to avoid the place.

President Adams stayed home in Massachusetts, Vice-
President Jefferson was at Monticello, and Secretary of State
Marshall was acting head of the government through the summer. Since no sane man would risk the health of his wife and
family by bringing them to Washington, he was without Polly,
and lived at a boarding house. From an improvised office in
the incomplete Capitol he managed the affairs of state, making most decisions on his own because an exchange of letters
with President Adams took as long as two weeks.

Marshall instructed America's envoys, carried on diplomatic transactions with other nations of the world, wrestled
over problems with France, England and the Barbary pirates,
handled Federal job-seekers, recommended appointments to

office, and spent his spare time writing the annual message President Adams would deliver to Congress when it convened. He made one quick trip to Virginia to see Polly and to argue a lawsuit and then hurried back to Washington. Here, in October, he received the treaty with France that had been approved by Napoleon, who had driven a hard bargain with the new American envoys to Paris. The French leader had made few concessions and Marshall did not like the terms but he realized they were the price of preserving neutrality and advised ratification if it meant peace.

President and Mrs. Adams reluctantly arrived in Washington in the fall to begin their brief and uncomfortable residence in the unfinished President's Mansion, and members began gathering for the December session of Congress that would be the last one under Federalist control. With the Republicans about to take over the government, the Federalists had one stronghold they meant to keep. In the Federal courts, no Republican had yet become a judge, and the courts had been towers of political strength. The judges made no pretense of being politically impartial. They actively served the Federalists. In charges to grand juries and in the reading of decisions, Federal judges delivered violent political tirades from the bench that were widely reprinted in Federalist newspapers. Courtrooms rang with fiercely partisan statements in the voice of judicial authority.

Almost as soon as Congress met, the Federalists moved to expand the judicial system and fasten lasting control upon it so that branch of government would remain theirs. They introduced a court-packing bill that on the face of it was offered as a means of bringing the courts closer to the people, relieving overburdened judges, and clearing crowded dockets to speed decisions. It called for the creation of many new district courts and justices of the peace and the appointment of sixteen new circuit judges to relieve the Supreme Court Justices from circuit duty, and provided that after the next vacancy the Supreme Court should be reduced from six to five members in the hope of keeping Republicans from naming a Justice for a long time to come.

But before Congress could get down to debating the proposed bill, there was a vacancy on the Supreme Court. Chief Justice Oliver Ellsworth, suffering from kidney trouble and the gout which an extended vacation at spas in the south of France had failed to improve, resigned for reasons of health. President Adams hastened to fill his place and in mid-December nominated treaty-maker John Jay, the first man to serve as Chief Justice, to take his old position again at the head of the Supreme Court.

But Jay, then Governor of New York, had no desire to accept. He believed that from its very start the Federal court system had been set up on a faulty basis rather than upon "principles of sound policy" and that it had never been placed "on a proper footing." The Supreme Court, in his opinion, had become such an insignificant branch of government that it never would amount to much. Jay wrote President Adams:

"I left the bench perfectly convinced that under a system so defective, it would not obtain the energy, weight, and dignity which are essential to its affording due support to the national government, nor acquire the public confidence and respect which, as the last resort of justice in the nation, it should possess."

Adams had to withdraw the nomination. He called Marshall into his office, showed him Jay's letter, and asked him, "Who shall I nominate now?" Marshall made some suggestions, but the President turned them down and after a moment's hesitation said, "I believe I must nominate you." According to Marshall, "I had never even thought of it. I was pleased as well as surprised . . ."

He didn't want public life, but this was a position in the

profession of law, and the short Court terms in Washington
still would give him most of the year free to be with his family
in Richmond. It was a lifetime appointment, not a temporary
position, and one that would both suit his best talents and
challenge them. He accepted on the spot.

The next day John Marshall was nominated the fourth
Chief Justice of the United States, succeeding to the office that
had been held in turn by John Jay, John Rutledge, and Oliver
Ellsworth during the Supreme Court's first twelve years of
feeble existence. Marshall's nomination was confirmed within
a week, only five days before the opening of the February
term of the Court. But President Adams insisted that he also
remain in the cabinet through the last weeks of his administration, so Marshall was Chief Justice and Secretary of State
at the same time.

Most of the country was less interested in Marshall's appointment than in the startling results of the Presidential
election. Republicans had won a sweeping victory and Jefferson clearly was the man the people wanted for President, but
because of the voting system there was a chance that the Republican Vice-Presidential candidate, New York's suave political boss, Aaron Burr, might be chosen President instead of
Jefferson.

Electoral College balloting for President and Vice-President
then was not separate. Each elector voted for two men and the
man who got the most votes became President, while the second highest became Vice-President. Republicans planned to
have a few electors split their votes so Jefferson would get the
most, but there was a slip-up in arrangements and every Republican elector voted for the same two candidates. When the
electoral votes were counted they showed the first and only
tie for President in American history. Both Jefferson and Burr
got seventy-three votes each.

Because of the dispute, the Constitution was amended a few

years later to provide that each elector must cast a separate ballot for President and Vice-President. But at the time, since neither Jefferson nor Burr had a majority, the election was thrown into the House of Representatives for a decision as required by the Constitution. And the House was dominated by Jefferson's political enemies, the Federalists, some of whom so thoroughly hated him that they would do anything to keep him from becoming President. Extreme Federalists in the House joined Burr's followers in an attempt to elect him instead of Jefferson.

There were rumors that Marshall favored Burr and that a deal had been made that if Burr got the Presidency he would keep Marshall as Secretary of State. Hamilton, who thought Burr would be an even worse calamity for the nation as President than Jefferson, fought the plot being hatched by the Federalists in Congress and appealed to Marshall to help block it by throwing his influence to Jefferson.

Marshall answered that he meant to keep his hands off. He wrote Hamilton that "I cannot bring myself to aid Mr. Jefferson" because he "appears to me to be a man who will . . . sap the fundamental principles of the government." On the other hand, while he was not well acquainted with Burr, "my preference would certainly not be for him." Under any circumstances, he would not remain as Secretary of State for any Republican President. "I can take no part in this business," he wrote. His present situation kept him "from using any influence . . . in support of either gentleman."

As the balloting in the House began on February 11, 1801, rumors spread through the excited capital that troops were forming in Pennsylvania for a people's march on Washington to enforce Jefferson's election. There were still wilder tales that Marshall, as Chief Justice, might appoint a Federalist President if the voting deadlock could not be broken, or that the House might choose Marshall himself as a compromise President.

For six days and thirty-five ballots, the battle went on in the House with no majority. But Hamilton's appeals to more moderate Federalists that "the public good must be paramount to every private consideration" had effect. On the seventh day, by prearrangement, enough Federalists cast blank ballots to give Jefferson ten of the sixteen states and the Presidency.

While Federalists in the House were battling over Jefferson, the Federalist Senate passed the Judiciary Bill. President Adams, with Marshall's help, raced to fill the new courts with good Federalists before Jefferson was inaugurated. Working against time, Adams made his appointments in batches and rushed them to the Senate, where they got quick confirmation. Two days before Jefferson became President all the newly created places on the Federal bench, high and low, had been filled.

Marshall spent almost all his last hours as Secretary of State writing out and signing commissions for new judges and court clerks. He stayed at his desk until nine o'clock the night before Jefferson's inauguration, working to complete the paper work until nearly the last minute of Adams' Presidency expired. Federalists felt they were saving the courts from the destruction Jefferson was to bring upon the national government, but to Republicans the whole thing seemed like a power grab. In a rage, Republican newspapers denounced the new court appointees as "midnight judges."

At noon the next day, no longer Secretary of State, Marshall went to the small Senate chamber as Chief Justice to swear Thomas Jefferson into office as the third President of the United States. As the two Virginians faced each other, Marshall held out the Bible to his red-haired cousin and Jefferson placed his hand upon it and repeated the oath to "preserve, protect and defend the Constitution of the United States."

Both now considered that their responsibility, but each with a different philosophy of that basic law. Jefferson would demand a strict interpretation as he sought to safeguard the rights of the common man against autocratic government; Marshall would interpret it liberally to strengthen national government, to establish the powers and durability of the Supreme Court, and to give the bare bones of the Constitution itself flesh, blood and muscle.

After swearing him into office, Marshall took his seat to the left of Jefferson, with Vice-President Burr at his right, and strained forward to listen to the inaugural address the new President read in such a low voice few of the thirty-two Senators could hear him. Public speaking was not among Jefferson's many talents, but what he said impressed Marshall as being "well-judged and conciliatory." Instead of the revolutionary call to arms many Federalists feared, Jefferson's speech was a lofty appeal for national unity. "Every difference of opinion is not a difference of principle," Jefferson said. "We are all Republicans; we are all Federalists."

But while Marshall approved Jefferson's plea, he expected no real truce. Since the courts were the last stronghold of the Federalists, it was obvious to Marshall that Jefferson would seek to diminish their power. Marshall was determined to strengthen the Supreme Court against Republican attack, to make it more important, not less important, in the structure of government.

As things stood when he became Chief Justice, the Supreme Court could hardly be less important than it was. Among the three co-ordinate branches of government, it was a poor third, weak, neglected, and all but ignored. Even the planners of Washington's public buildings had forgotten about it. They had constructed the magnificent Capitol for Congress, the Mansion for the President, but had never gotten a home for the Court off the drawing board. On the day Marshall was nominated for Chief Justice, the District Commissioners asked Congress if it would be kind enough to accommodate the Supreme Court "with a room in the Capitol to hold its sessions until further provisions shall be made." He held Court for the next seven years in a twenty-four-foot Senate committee room.

Until Marshall's time, the Justices of the Supreme Court, although proud of their proclaimed independent status, actually were far from independent. They served the Federalist Presidents, and as the political parties developed became outspoken party men. Most Federalists had never thought of the Court as really non-partisan. Judges, like all other officeholders, were expected to support the administration. But Marshall, unlike the three Chief Justices before him, was faced with an opposing administration.

He was and he remained the most political of men. His great decisions were Federalist political acts. Within the fortress he built of the Supreme Court, Marshall became the real leader of the Federalists. For a quarter of a century, as "the last of the Federalists," he kept alive the influence of a party that died. His Federalist decrees threw up an almost impregnable legal barricade around the Union and the business interests that benefited from it.

Yet he also saw from the start that to make the Supreme Court strong and effective he had to make it truly independent, respected for its judicial authority. He worked to lift the Court above the strife of the immediate political arena and to set it apart and aloof from day-to-day political controversy. In self-defense against the attacks he expected Republicans to make, as well as a matter of principle, Marshall set the precedent that a Chief Justice, at least publicly, should remain strictly non-partisan.

He meant to divorce himself and the Court from involvement with the other branches of the government, separate it from the Presidency and Congress. The attitude of the Chief

Justice, Marshall decided, should be one of profound silence on public affairs. Through the years he became increasingly strict about it, even to the point of refusing to vote in national elections so as to keep his personal preference for President unknown.

Within the Court, he acted to reduce controversy over its decisions. Marshall changed the custom of letting the Justices read opinions in turn. As Chief Justice he assumed the function of becoming the voice of the Court. He strengthened his own authority by delivering nearly all major opinions himself. Other Justices might read dissenting opinions, but the final ruling usually was read by Marshall. He wanted the public to know that although the Justices might differ, when the Court spoke it was as a body, and that what it said was the law.

There were few serious differences of opinion among Marshall's fellow Justices when he took charge of the Court. They were a politically happy family, staunch Federalists all. Sixty-eight-year-old William Cushing, oldest among them, had been serving since he was appointed to the first Supreme Court by George Washington. An imposing, erudite, long-nosed New Englander who wore a big curly wig, Cushing had once turned down a chance to become Chief Justice, preferring to remain just a member of the Court.

Samuel Chase, nearing sixty, was a bullying rage of a man, coarse-mannered, aggressive and vindictive. A signer of the Declaration of Independence, he had been in his youth a fiery patriot who helped swing Maryland to Revolution. Seldom known to let the law get in the way of his political convictions, Chase used the courts as his sounding board in lashing out at all who opposed Federalists.

As a trial judge he could be terrifying, and had been among the fiercest in applying the Sedition Laws, for which Republicans branded him a tyrant. But Chase also was an extremely able lawyer, former chief judge of his state court, and a writer of brilliant and influential opinions that made him leader of the Supreme Court until Marshall's rising genius eclipsed him.

Irish-born Justice William Paterson, in his late fifties, was a scholarly former senator and governor of New Jersey who had played a leading role in the framing of the Constitution. Alfred Moore of North Carolina, on the Court only little more than a year and probably least influential in its decisions, was a bald, trim-figured man of forty-five, the same age as Marshall. Closest to Marshall as a personal friend was Bushrod Washington, nephew and heir of George Washington, modest despite his great family prestige. A pleasant, articulate young man, he had little interest in party politics but had a genuine interest in law.

By tradition the Justices came from various sections of the country because that was the only practical way they could carry out the hardest part of their duty, which was not to sit on the Supreme Bench during the semi-annual sessions in Washington, but to ride the circuit. The law had provided that the Supreme Court Justices must hold circuit courts once a year in every district in the United States, two Justices sitting together with the district judge to make a court of three. Riding circuit was an ordeal of physical endurance that ruined the health of some Justices and was blamed for the death of at least one of them. In addition, it meant that in the Supreme Court they would receive cases they had already ruled upon in lower court.

Marshall and his Court were relieved temporarily of the killing burden of circuit riding by the Federalist Judiciary Bill, passed at the time he became Chief Justice. It was partly to correct such conditions that sixteen new circuit judges were created. Although it didn't last long when Jefferson and the Republicans got to work on it, Marshall started as Chief Justice expecting to have plenty of free time.

He would have to consider cases, of course, but much of

the law reading and preparation could be done at home in Richmond. There were no important cases on the Supreme Court docket when he took over. Twice a year, in June and December, he would have to come to Washington for a few weeks to hold sessions, and share boarding house accommodations in convivial stag company with his fellow Justices while he took care of whatever business the Court might have.

He was so confident that most of the year would be his that he undertook a second job and agreed to write the official biography of George Washington. Bushrod Washington infected him with enthusiasm for the idea. From the time George Washington died, Bushrod had been besieged by publishers who wanted an authorized biography. As custodian of his uncle's papers, he offered to turn them over to Marshall and help with the work for a share in the profits. Marshall expected to get enough out of it to more than pay off what he owed for the Fairfax lands. It seemed a chance to lift himself out of debt and at the same time provide the world with the definitive life story of the man whose memory he treasured.

Having never written anything but law briefs, speeches, official documents and some unpublished poetry, he was blissfully ignorant of the work involved. Although he hadn't yet glanced at the bins of letters and papers Washington had left, or attempted to make an outline, he estimated he could turn out several volumes of about five hundred pages each in about a year. For that, he and Bushrod wanted $150,000. The publishers suggested it was unlikely the books would earn one-fifth of that. Negotiations dragged on. By the time Marshall had signed the contract, he had become more cautious and refused to set a date for delivering the manuscript. The first volume took three years and the whole endeavor became a grinding task and a source of pressures, complaints and complications for a good part of his life. Stuck with it, he struggled on, writing the original and revising new editions, now and then and when he could, with poor results and little satisfaction.

But that literary drudgery was still in the future in June, 1801, when John Marshall heard his first case as Chief Justice of the Supreme Court. Entered on the docket as *Talbot vs. Seeman,* it involved adventure on the high seas during the undeclared naval war between the United States and France. Captain Silas Talbot of the frigate *Constitution* claimed salvage fees from the owner of the German merchant ship *Amelia,* captured by the French and then rescued by the American ship, which brought the German vessel to safe harbor in New York. The owners refused to pay, claiming the *Amelia* had not been salvaged from any normal perils of the sea.

Such questions of international law were raised as whether the undeclared war with France actually was a war and whether the *Amelia* was legally in danger. Marshall answered yes to both questions. His opinion was based on common sense reasoning that the owners never would have seen the *Amelia* or its cargo again if it hadn't been saved from the French who had seized it in the Caribbean and were sailing off with it as a prize. In the true sense, he held, that was salvage, and Captain Talbot should get his reward.

The Court dealt with a few other cases and Marshall was then free to return to Richmond. He spent part of his time at home reading history for the contemplated biography of Washington. When he returned to the capital for the December term of Court, arrangements for the book were practically settled and he looked forward to getting down to work on it. But the free time he expected was about to go up in smoke.

President Jefferson and the Republicans were preparing to launch their attack on the courts. Jefferson sounded the call in his first message to the Congress now controlled by his own party, sharply criticizing the Federalist Judiciary Act of the previous winter. He charged that the increase in courts and judges was extravagant and unnecessary.

The first skirmish in the battle began when four men appeared in the Supreme Court to present claims to positions as justices of peace in the District of Columbia. One of them was named William Marbury, and because of the suit they filed his name would go down in history. They raised a point of law Chief Justice Marshall would answer in a way that forever changed the place the Supreme Court had in the government of the United States.

JOHN MARSHALL had left some papers on his desk in those hectic last hours as Secretary of State when he was signing commissions for new judges appointed by President Adams. James Madison had found them in Marshall's old office when he took over as President Jefferson's new Secretary of State. The papers were commissions for forty-two men to become justices of the peace in the District of Columbia, commissions that had been legally signed and sealed but never delivered to the men who were appointed.

President Jefferson decided that was more justices than the muddy little District of Columbia could ever use, especially since the men would be Federalist justices, so he told Madison to throw away seventeen of the commissions and forget about them. According to later testimony, the papers apparently were burned in a fireplace of the State Department office instead of being delivered to the men appointed by President Adams and approved by Congress. Since the job as a justice of peace was not very important, most of the men who failed to get their commissions grumbled a little but decided there was no point in trying to fight.

William Marbury and three others went before the Supreme

Court and asked for a writ of mandamus to compel Secretary of State Madison to give them their commissions. There were hints that Marbury and his friends were encouraged to make an issue of it by the Federalists who hoped that the threat of Court action might worry Jefferson and the Republicans enough so they would think twice before launching an all-out battle against the court system. If so, the threat failed to work.

Marshall, as the new Chief Justice, followed the usual procedure in such cases and issued a routine order in December, 1801, for a show of cause as to why the writ of mandamus should not be issued. It was routine except that it was directed against Secretary of State Madison, calling upon him to explain why he had never delivered the commissions.

Republicans were outraged. They called Marshall's order a challenge by the Supreme Court of Presidential authority and an attempt to "interfere" with Jefferson's administration. The suit of *Marbury vs. Madison* was left pending. But Jefferson and his Republican Congress began their full war against the court system with a sweeping first victory. Early in January, 1802, Senate Republicans launched a successful drive to repeal the Federalist Judiciary Act of the year before.

Charging that the Federalists had created useless courts and unnecessary judges, and declaring that the power to create a court carried with it the power to abolish that court, the Republican Senators overrode all opposition and by a strictly party vote pushed through the repeal. The House, after weeks of debate and the first midnight session in its history, went along with the Senate.

The Republican Congress did away with the new Federalist circuit court judges simply by abolishing the jobs to which they had been appointed for life under the Constitution. Congress also struck directly at the Supreme Court. It reduced Court sessions to only one a year, thereby eliminating the June term of Court and putting off its next term until 1803. By silencing the Court for nearly a year, the Republicans kept it from making any immediate rulings, in the hope that by the time the Court did meet again the excitement would die down and everybody would accept what had been done.

During the debates in Congress, some of which Marshall attended as a spectator, speakers explored the power of the Supreme Court to rule on acts of Congress and raised the pending challenge of the *Marbury vs. Madison* suit. But Republicans considered those side issues at the time. They accomplished what they wanted to do, which was to shake some of the Federalist strength out of the courts.

Federalists gloomily foresaw an end to the entire national court system. Jefferson was known to believe that each state, as well as each branch of government, should be its own interpreter of the Constitution as it affected their activities, and that in certain cases the President himself should have authority to decide whether laws were constitutional.

The *Washington Federalist* predicted that the next Republican move would be to repeal the law that had created the Supreme Court. That was an extreme view, and not even ardent Republicans had suggested going that far, but it reflected the fears of many Federalists that Jefferson meant to reduce the power of the courts, and particularly the Supreme Court, to zero.

By temporarily all but abolishing the Supreme Court, in silencing it for a year, the Republican Congress had given Marshall and the other Justices something of a vacation. But by doing away with the new circuit court judges, they had put the task of circuit riding upon the Supreme Court Justices again. The new law assigned them to the circuit courts singly instead of in pairs, so that each Justice would have less territory to cover, but it still meant rough travel over long distances and a burden of extra court work.

Marshall's first reaction was to refuse to obey the Republican Congress. He privately asked the other Justices how they felt about it, pointing out that under the Constitution they were appointed only as judges of the Supreme Court, and questioning whether Congress had a right to reassign them to circuit duties. Some of his fellow Justices agreed with him, but others shied away from challenging Congress so directly, so he abandoned the plan and all the Justices obeyed the new law. He sat as a circuit judge in Richmond in the fall of 1802 and accepted the fate that would take him circuit riding from there into North Carolina.

He bore his vexations, outwardly cheerful if somewhat absent-minded, as he tried to think out what the Court should do about the challenge to its Constitutional powers. Driving himself over the back roads in a battered gig to make the rounds of his circuit, he wrote Polly from Raleigh, North Carolina, that "you will laugh . . . when you hear the calamities that have befallen me."

First, he told her, he discovered that fifteen silver dollars he had in his coat "had worn through the various mendings" of his pocket "and sought their liberty in the sands of Carolina." Then, when he unpacked his clothes to dress for court, he found "to my astonishment and grief . . . I had no pair of breeches." All the tailors in town were too busy to make him a pair in a hurry so he had to spend his days in court in rough and informal riding clothes instead of the gentlemanly "breeches" a judge was expected to wear.

Such stories about him amused the countryside. Tales were told of his jogging about, looking so unkempt that strangers in taverns where he stopped sometimes mistook him for a loafer and were surprised by his unexpected discourses on politics, philosophy and poetry. In Richmond, a near-sighted woman, noting only his rough clothing, mistook him for a yard man she was expecting to come shake out her rugs. Another time a young dandy tossed him a quarter to carry a live turkey from market, and was stunned when he was later told that the man who had laughed, pocketed the coin, and meekly trotted behind him carrying the squawking bird happened to be the Chief Justice of the United States.

Marshall delighted at times in playing up to such pranks, and also in the horseshoe-pitching contests and general hearty company of other men, but at home he was a quieter man. Seated at his favorite place for study, on a big bench under an oak tree in the yard, with books and papers spread beside him, he gave the family to understand that he was not to be disturbed. But first the youngest child would edge toward him to find a place on the bench, and then another, until he soon had made room for all. He never could resist such intrusions.

When Polly felt overcome with the household duties her illness made it difficult for her to manage, he sometimes sent her out for a carriage ride while he knotted a bandanna about his head, rolled up his sleeves and house-managed a thorough cleaning job in her absence. Strangers who saw Polly only as a neurotic semi-invalid found it hard to understand his continuing devotion, but it satisfied him to give himself to her comfort.

He and Polly spent part of that summer on a brief trip to Oak Hill. His father had died in Kentucky only months before and there was sadness for Marshall in going back to the Virginia mountain estate, now his, that had been the home he had shared with his father. But the mountains also gave him a sense of renewal and a freshening of mind, as they always had, and it was sorely needed. He also needed courage for what he was about to do.

Marshall had become increasingly alarmed over the waning power of the Judicial branch of government under Republican attack. Congress had assumed a free hand in dealing with the courts as it pleased, the President seemed ready to ignore laws he didn't approve, and some states were openly threatening to decide for themselves what laws to accept. The Supreme Court was held in low esteem and the nation had been little impressed with its wisdom, dignity or force. Instead of the strong, independent and stabilizing balance it should be in national government, the Judiciary was fast becoming a pawn to the other branches.

In Marshall's mind there never was a question about whether the Supreme Court could say with final authority what the law of the land was. Although no specific words of the Constitution gave such power to the Court, he had accepted it since the Constitution was first written as the Court's right to examine the laws and annul those it found unconstitutional. He had asserted that right himself in the Virginia legislature, in the Virginia ratifying convention, and had found it clearly stated to his satisfaction in Alexander Hamilton's *Federalist* papers.

Most Americans, when they weren't aroused by partisan politics, assumed the Court had such power. Over the years the courts had been asked to declare laws unconstitutional for various reasons, and there was nothing basically new in the idea. Since Jefferson's rise to power, all the arguments had been made over and over, and Marshall had no new thought to contribute that had not been voiced by hundreds of other men.

But as Chief Justice he held the position of authority and he felt it had become his duty to assert it, boldly, clearly, and for all America to understand. Marshall also knew he was a political thorn in Jefferson's side, one that Jefferson meant to remove if he could. Even his last-minute appointment as Chief Justice by President Adams had thwarted Jefferson's hope of appointing his own man, Judge Spencer Roane of Virginia, as Chief Justice. If Jefferson found or made an excuse to impeach Marshall, Roane still would take his place. Even without that, illness or death might provide Court vacancies for Jefferson to fill, to break the solidarity of the Court. The need for the Court to act, to make the nation know it could and would assume its full power, was urgent.

How the Court could act had been Marshall's year-long problem. It could not simply pronounce itself the final arbiter of the Constitution; it could act only if a case came to it that legally justified and technically required such a pronouncement. The Court was not supposed to reach out for trumped-up cases to decide, just to voice its views. But reach out was what Marshall finally did, although not beyond the docket. The case of *Marbury vs. Madison* was still pending and, with a vision clearer than anybody outside the Court guessed, he reached for that.

It had by then dwindled to an almost insignificant case. Even Marbury and the three others who had brought the suit to gain their commissions as justices of the peace had lost interest in it. The terms for which they had been appointed were half-expired, the fees were small, and the work was being handled by the District of Columbia's other justices, so there was little in it for them if they finally did get the jobs.

That was unlikely in any event, because Jefferson's administration probably would ignore any Court ruling to produce the commissions. From a practical point of view, nobody thought it would make much difference how the Court disposed of *Marbury vs. Madison*. It had become pretty much a moot question, interesting only because of the legal technicalities and what might be made of them politically.

Chief Justice Marshall was in the awkward position of having to decide a case in which he had been personally involved as Secretary of State, a suit that in fact never would have been brought if he had seen to it in the first place that the commissions he signed and sealed actually were delivered to Marbury and the others. He had to be very circumspect in handling it, more so because Jefferson's administration had made it freshly clear that the Republicans were hunting for the slightest excuse to impeach judges.

Marshall and his fellow Justices had hardly settled into their Washington boarding house to prepare for the Supreme Court term that was to open in February, 1803, and break the year's silence that had been imposed upon them by Congress, before they were given warning of what was to come. Five days before they opened Court, Jefferson sent Congress a message asking it to look into the conduct of Federal District Judge John Pickering of New Hampshire, and started action to remove him from the bench. Washington gossip was alive with rumors that Jefferson also was planning to strike at Marshall's own Court associate, Justice Samuel Chase, and that if Chase could be impeached, Marshall himself would be next.

But in the boarding house, during the evenings that he and the other Justices spent in informal discussions of cases that were to come before the Court, Marshall raised some startlingly new questions about *Marbury vs. Madison*. He had conceived a daring approach, entirely different from any thinking about the case that had gone before. The Court could reach no decision, of course, before the case had been heard, but in talking together over dinner and afterwards six good friends could explore the possibilities. There was nothing revolutionary in the suggestion Marshall made to them that an act of Congress might be declared unconstitutional. But the pretext he had devised was his original contribution. It was a plan forced by the emergency, an extraordinary and novel plan, and the other Justices gave it their unanimous approval.

It was almost as a comedy that the Supreme Court hearings on *Marbury vs. Madison* began. Marshall had to sit, straightfaced and solemn, listening as Chief Justice to arguments over whether the commissions he knew he had signed as Secretary of State had ever been signed. With Secretary of State Madison ignoring the proceedings and the Republican Senate refusing to produce its records, it wasn't easy for lawyers to prove the basic fact that any commissions had ever existed. Then came the question as to what had happened to them. Marshall himself was curious about that, since the last time he had seen them they had been on his own desk.

But it now seemed that Madison hadn't gotten rid of the papers personally when he came to take over Marshall's old office. During the first weeks of Jefferson's Presidency, Madison had been away from Washington and Attorney General Levi Lincoln had served as acting Secretary of State. Probably Lincoln had thrown Marbury's commission into the fireplace to destroy it. Lincoln happened to be in court because as Attorney General he was defending the government in the case of *Marbury vs. Madison*. So Chief Justice Marshall put the direct question to Attorney General Lincoln from the bench and asked what *had* become of the missing papers.

The Attorney General of the United States pleaded the Fifth Amendment. Since the Court might hold that the destruction of the papers was a criminal offense, Attorney General Lincoln quite properly took advantage of the Fifth Amendment's privilege and refused to answer on the grounds "that I might incriminate myself." Marshall told him he was within his rights and went on with the hearings.

When the hearings ended, everybody thought Marshall and the Court were faced with a dilemma from which there was no escape. If he and the other Justices, in the face of political threats, failed to assert their independence as guardians of the Constitution who were above intimidation by the President and the Congress, they would be admitting the Jeffersonian doctrine that the Supreme Court had no power to rule on the acts of other branches of government.

On the other hand, if the Court commanded Secretary Madison to deliver the commission to Marbury, it would bring the Executive and Judicial departments into direct conflict. Madison probably would refuse to obey and the Court would have no power to enforce its mandate.

There seemed no alternative except for the Court to dismiss the application and admit it was powerless, or to issue the writ and put itself in the predicament of being unable to enforce it. But Marshall had found an alternative. He and the other Justices reached a surprisingly swift decision.

His lanky figure covered by his black robe, Marshall took his place at the head of the Court, leaning forward as he read his opinion. Sweeping his right arm before him from time to time in a circular gesture of emphasis, he spoke for an hour and a half on the question of whether Marbury was legally entitled to his commission.

That was the first part of his opinion and Marshall discreetly held it to the level of a judgment made in passing. It amounted to a severe lecture to Jefferson on the ethics of disregarding the Constitution, given as the collective view of the Court, but not binding. It was "decidedly the opinion of the Court," he said, that Marbury had been legally and rightfully appointed a justice of peace, and "to withhold his commission ... is an act deemed by the Court not warranted by law. ..."

But Marshall then went on to another question, which was whether the Supreme Court had a right to issue a writ of mandamus. And for his surprising answer to that, he reached all the way back to the Judiciary Act of the first Congress of the United States in 1789. A section of that act empowered the Court to issue such writs and it had been accepted until then without question. Marbury and his lawyers had brought their suit to the Court on that basis, but it was upon it that Marshall now built an ingenious paradox.

He had held that Marbury certainly was entitled to his commission and that President Jefferson should give it to him, but he now added that Marbury had come to the wrong place to seek a remedy. Marbury would have to take his problem somewhere else because the Court could not force the President or Secretary Madison to deliver the commission. The reason the Court could do nothing about it, in Marshall's opinion, was because the Constitution denied it the jurisdiction to do so.

Marshall ruled that the first Congress had violated the bounds of the Constitution by giving the Court power to issue such writs, because the Constitution itself clearly limited the kinds of cases on which the Court could act directly without an appeal from a lower court. The Constitution nowhere gave Congress the right to enlarge the original jurisdiction of the Court. Congress therefore had acted wrongly in making the law in Section 13 of the Judiciary Act of 1789. He said:

"The powers of the legislature are defined and limited; and that those limits may not be mistaken or forgotten, the Constitution is written. To what purpose are powers limited ... if these limits may, at any time, be passed by those intended to be restrained? The distinction between a government with limited and unlimited powers is abolished if those limits do not confine the persons on whom they are imposed. ...

"It is emphatically the province and duty of the Judicial Department to say what the law is," he went on. "Those who apply the rule to particular cases must, of necessity, expound and interpret that rule. If two laws conflict with each other, the courts must decide on the operation of each. So, if a law be in opposition to the Constitution ... the Constitution and not such ordinary act must govern the case to which they both apply. ... The judicial power of the United States is extended to all cases arising under the Constitution."

As he read on through the many pages of his complex

opinion, declaring that "a law repugnant to the Constitution is void," listeners slowly realized that for the first time the Supreme Court was presuming to find an act of Congress unconstitutional. But Marshall's genius had so carefully chosen the way of doing it that neither the President nor the Congress could do anything about it.

He was asserting the complete independence of the Judiciary, and at the same time lecturing the Executive branch on its duty, but without giving the President a chance to defy a Court order. He was telling the Republican Congress that the Court might declare its laws no laws at all unless they stayed within the bounds of the Constitution, but he was ruling on a law passed by a Federalist Congress fourteen years before. He was actually limiting the Court's own area of jurisdiction, but by doing so was giving the Court its greatest power.

Marbury had his suit dismissed without getting the writ and Madison never gave him his commission as justice of peace, but Marbury no longer cared. What was more important to the United States was that Chief Justice Marshall had answered, and forever, the question of what branch of government had final decision in interpreting the Constitution. His opinion had set a landmark so high that the future would take bearings from it, and so enduring that it would stand through all the years.

He had stunned Thomas Jefferson into infuriated if temporary silence. But he had not silenced those who would attack the Supreme Court, then and also through the years to come.

13

JOHN MARSHALL was a worried man in February, 1805, and had reason to be. Thomas Jefferson, at the crest of his popularity after being overwhelmingly re-elected President, was starting at the top with a "judicial reform" to sweep the courts of Federalist judges who opposed Republican policies.

The Supreme Court itself was to be brought to trial in the person of Marshall's fellow Justice Samuel Chase. If Chase could be removed from the bench for having political views against the party in power, the precedent would be set for the conviction of others. It was no secret that the man Jefferson really wanted to oust was Chief Justice Marshall.

Jefferson's personal spokesman in the Senate, William Giles of Virginia, openly scorned the idea of "an independent judiciary." He said that if the Supreme Court Justices dared "as they had done, to declare the acts of Congress unconstitutional . . . it was the undoubted right of the House to impeach them and of the Senate to remove them for giving such opinions." Giles maintained that "removal by impeachment was nothing more than a declaration by Congress to this effect: 'You hold dangerous opinions. . . .' "

The recent impeachment trial by Congress of Federal

District Judge John Pickering had failed to provide the Republicans with the precedent they wanted to remove judges for their political opinions. The House had tried Pickering, and members of the Senate, acting as his judges, had found him "guilty as charged." But the verdict had side-stepped the question of removing him from office for non-criminal acts because petitions were presented that Judge Pickering was drunk and insane.

Jefferson, impatient over the Pickering case, complained that the "Constitution ought to be altered so that the President," with the simple approval of both houses of Congress, "should be authorized to remove a judge from office."

Justice Chase, the blazing old patriot of Revolution, had never been one to hide his Federalist views. He had been high-handed in rulings, openly rude to Republican lawyers and defendants, had scathingly called the Jeffersonians a "mobocracy" that would bring the nation to ruin, and had been their primary target of rage since the Sedition trials. Finally he had spoken out once too often and had given the Republicans what they believed was good reason to have him impeached.

While making the rounds of his circuit, Chase had used the occasion of charging a grand jury in Baltimore to warn that the Republicans had brought "a mighty mischief upon us" that would progress "until peace and order, freedom and prosperity, shall be destroyed." An angered Maryland Republican had sent President Jefferson a newspaper clipping of Chase's remarks and Jefferson had promptly shot a note to his leaders in the House to ask. "Ought this seditious and official attack on the principles of our Constitution . . . go unpunished?" In his note Jefferson said that as President he personally "should not interfere," but that the public would look to Congress "for the necessary measures."

The House impeached Chase on eight counts, accusing him of almost everything that anybody had ever complained about since he became a Justice of the Supreme Court. In the eight articles laid before the Senators who would act as his judges, Chase was charged among other things with "oppressive conduct" during the Sedition trials, with forcing a false jury verdict, and with delivering "an intemperate and inflammatory harangue" to the grand jury at Baltimore. The impeachment said he was guilty of using the bench as "an electioneering partisan" to excite "odium . . . against the government."

Marshall could see the Republican finger pointing right at him. Although he was not in any way accused, he also would face questioning at the trial, as a witness called upon to explain his views of such judicial conduct. If he criticized his fellow Justice, he would give the Jeffersonians fresh ammunition for their propaganda against the Court; if he defended Chase's conduct, he would give them more reason to attack him personally.

The month-long impeachment trial began February 4, 1805, in a Senate chamber the Republicans had turned more into a theater than a courtroom. It was aglow with theatrical color. Two rows of benches where the thirty-four Senators would sit as the judges of Samuel Chase, impeached for "high crimes and misdemeanors," were draped with scarlet cloth in imitation of a British court of high inquiry. Covered with green, three more tiers of benches for members of the House extended from the wall toward the center of the room. In a separate enclosure were the members of Jefferson's cabinet.

People fought for seats in the jammed visitors' gallery and beneath it was another green-covered temporary gallery, flanked by boxes, filled with invited guests of Congress and their ladies. At the sides were two blue-colored stalls, one for defense lawyers and the other for those who would present the House charges against Chase. Marshall and his associate Justices were among the spectators, but conscious that they and the Court they represented were almost as much on trial as Chase.

Presiding over the Senatorial court was a man under indictment in two states for murder, Aaron Burr, who had resumed his duties as Vice-President of the United States after his fatal duel with Alexander Hamilton. His reputation ruined and his career shattered, the short, pallid-faced and elegantly dressed ex-boss of New York's Republican party braved the stares of those who condemned him for the exchange of dueling shots six months before, when he and Hamilton had met at dawn on the New Jersey shore of the Hudson River. Hamilton's pistol had fired into the air, but Burr had mortally wounded Hamilton, who died the next day.

They had been enemies for years, as young Revolutionary Army officers, rival lawyers, and savage political opponents, but the direct quarrel which brought on the duel was Burr's loss of a bid for the Governorship of New York in 1804. Burr blamed Hamilton, who controlled Federalist votes, for that, and for writing letters in which he called Burr "a dangerous man."

Bankrupt both politically and financially, Burr had sought the governorship after being forced out of power nationally in the Republican party. Although he had done more than any other political leader to swing the balance of votes that made Jefferson President in 1800, the dispute over the election in the House had left Jefferson suspicious. He believed Burr had plotted to take the Presidency from him and deeply and forever mistrusted him. Jefferson squeezed him out of the Vice-Presidency in 1804 by choosing George Clinton of New York, Burr's former ally turned enemy, instead of Burr as his second-term running mate.

Dueling was a well-accepted custom as a means of settling political arguments but the public had turned in outrage against Burr, branding him a "scoundrel who killed Hamilton like a dog." As a fugitive charged with murder, Burr had fled as far as the swamps of Georgia before returning to Washington to serve out the last weeks of his term as Vice-President.

Presiding now over the trial of Justice Chase, he was meticulous in manners and deportment, and he found himself briefly in favor with the Republicans again as they courted his good will with dinner parties and flattery. Even Jefferson managed to swallow his dislike of Burr for the length of the trial and to invite him to dinners at the Executive Mansion. It was Burr who had arranged the theatrical setting in the Senate, both to please the Republicans and in the hope of providing a dramatic background that would help him regain some of his lost prestige. But he handled the trial with a precise fairness that pleased both sides.

John Randolph of Roanoke, Jefferson's leader in the House, but already in dispute with him over some of his policies, was Chase's chief prosecutor. Childish-looking, soprano-voiced, his frail body raddled by unexplained disease, he also was a man of proven personal bravery. A distant cousin to both Marshall and Jefferson, the brilliant-minded Randolph was a master of sharp and withering sarcasm, and had become a figure of compelling power in the House.

Randolph opened the trial by skillfully contrasting Marshall's conduct on the bench in circuit court with the way Chase behaved. It was a clever approach, designed to win the support of moderate Senators, but Randolph also personally liked Marshall. Against the bullying of Chase, he pictured Marshall as a gentle-mannered, large-minded "enlightened man," who "gave the accused a fair trial according to law and usage." Fifty-two witnesses were examined, and when Randolph came to question Marshall among them, he again treated him with respect.

Without directly mentioning Marshall by name, Randolph

described his ideal of a judge as "firm indeed, but temperate, mild though unyielding, neither a blustering bravo nor a timid poltroon." In contrast he charged that Chase was not "fit to preside in a court of justice," that the accused was "today haughty, violent, imperious; tomorrow humble, penitent and submissive."

But for all of that, Randolph and others subjected Marshall to hard questioning, and tried time after time to force him to make some damaging criticism of Chase. Marshall was a nervous witness, evasive under obvious pressure, but he skillfully parried most of the questions. To some he answered that he did not "recollect precisely," and to others he objected that he was being asked to evaluate Chase's conduct rather than to state facts of which he had direct knowledge. He pointed out that "my practice while I was at the bar was very limited in criminal cases."

Yet he did admit that Chase had made some "unusual" rulings, that he had heard Chase apply "unusual epithets" to lawyers who appeared before him, and that perhaps Chase had been too abrupt at times in interrupting arguments or in refusing to hear testimony. Some of Marshall's answers were not favorable to Chase, but his questioners really got little from him.

Leading off in Chase's defense, after all the testimony had been taken, was attorney Joseph Hopkinson, who in addition to being an outstanding lawyer was the writer of the *President's March,* the song that had become popular as *Hail, Columbia!* Hopkinson struck to the center of the argument by charging that Chase's impeachment had been based on "a petty catalogue of frivolous occurrences."

Could a judge be impeached merely for "error, mistake or indiscretion?" he asked, and said that was "absurd!" Such action could be taken, under the terms clearly set forth in the Constitution, only for "an indictable offense."

The power of impeachment was not based on "opinion,

whim or caprice," Hopkinson declared. The Constitution limited it to such "high crimes" as treason, bribery or corruption, that were "well understood and defined" as acts "committed or omitted in violation of a *public* law." If a judge could be "condemned by the mere voice of prejudice," he argued, then no judge ever would dare to be firm, unbiased and independent.

Maryland's famed attorney general, the great Luther Martin, then took up Chase's defense. Considered the most celebrated lawyer of the age, Martin drew such crowds to the Capitol to hear him that the overflow jammed the corridors outside the Senate. Then in his sixties, and often drunk both in court and out, grown gray, shabby, near-sighted and absent-minded, he still was the acknowledged leader of the bar, as he had been for two generations.

Martin had been Chase's lifelong friend and he spoke for two days, from morning to night, holding the shifting crowds almost silent with his non-stop oratory. If he had come only to defend a friend, Martin said, he would not be so gravely concerned, but the trial was vital, not only to all living Americans but to posterity, because it would establish "a most important precedent as to future cases of impeachment."

If the Senate were to convict Chase on such "frivolous charges" as had been brought against him, he warned, "then you leave your judges and all your other officers at the mercy of the prevailing party." What Chase had been accused of, Martin declared, was "rather a violation of the principles of politeness, than the principles of law; rather the want of decorum, than the commission of a high crime and misdemeanor." He ridiculed the attempt to remove a Supreme Court Justice for his tone of voice, his language, his manner of bowing, his opinions and remarks, none of which were legally crimes within the meaning of the Constitution.

"We boast that ours is a government of laws," Martin said, "but how can it be unless the laws ... are sacredly and impartially, without regard to popularity, carried into execution?" Only independent judges could do this, and our "property, our liberty, our lives, can only be protected and secured by such judges. With this honorable court it remains, whether we shall *have* such judges!"

There were other attorneys, for and against Chase, and some brought Marshall's name into the hearings. He was among the tense spectators when the Senate convened shortly after noon on March 1, 1805, finally to reach its verdict on Chase's impeachment. As the eight articles were read and voted upon in turn, the vote on each was, "Not guilty."

Although all but nine of the Senators were Republicans, the majority agreed that no official should be removed by impeachment except for legally provable "high crimes and misdemeanors." They established the principle that judges must be protected from popular prejudice and the fluctuations of partisan feelings.

People didn't stop criticizing the courts, but political impeachments were halted and the threat of them was lifted. For the first time since he was appointed Chief Justice, Marshall felt secure at the head of the Supreme Court, with the knowledge that his opinions could not be used to impeach him. A crisis in America's history had passed and the courts could stand independent. But the judges also learned a lesson from the trial of Samuel Chase: that they must not mix law and politics on the bench.

President Jefferson had lost none of his political enmity toward Marshall, nor toward the court system he wished to reform, but he would no longer try to sweep the bench clean through impeachment. Jefferson privately told Senator William Plumer, a New Hampshire Federalist he was about to take into the Republican fold, that "impeachment is a farce which will not be tried again."

14

TALES OF a strange and mysterious adventure involving Aaron Burr began to reach John Marshall from friends in the Mississippi River country. The reports he received were conflicting and confusing, and nobody ever would be certain as to the real purpose of Burr's intrigues, then or afterwards. From the letters Marshall got, he knew many people were becoming alarmed over Burr's activities, but he had no way of knowing that the former Vice-President of the United States soon would be charged with treason and that he would be called to sit as Burr's judge.

Marshall was more immediately concerned with problems of his own Court. The resignation of Justice Albert Moore because of ill health had given President Jefferson his first chance to fill a Supreme Court vacancy, and Marshall had feared the worst. But his worries were somewhat put at rest when Jefferson appointed William Johnson, who at thirty-two was the youngest man yet to serve on the Court.

Johnson, who had been a South Carolina judge, was a disciple of Jefferson's and could be expected to dissent from some of Marshall's opinions. But that was balanced by the fact that Johnson had studied law in the office of Marshall's friend, Charles Pinckney, and probably would be a sound constitutionalist. He also was young enough to withstand the hazards of circuit riding. Considering everything, Marshall wasn't too displeased by Jefferson's choice.

The first indications that Marshall had of really serious trouble developing around Burr's adventures was in reports from his brother-in-law in Kentucky, Senator Humphrey Marshall, and from Federal attorney Alexander Daviess, who had established a newspaper there, the *Western World*. Daviess had become so alarmed that he wrote to warn President Jefferson of Burr's "dangerous activities," but since Daviess was a Federalist the President discounted his letters as an attempt to stir up trouble for the Republicans.

Daviess then had his editors put together a sensational story intimating that Burr was a traitor. Other newspapers picked it up and enlarged upon it and news swiftly spread across the country that Burr was behind a movement to divide the Union and establish his own empire in the Southwest.

When Aaron Burr left the Capitol at the end of his term as Vice-President he was a broken man, burdened by debt, his reputation gone. Desperately seeking to recover his fame and fortune, he filled his mind with a dozen grandiose plans. He had come within a breath of being President and his ambition soared to new heights of glory and renown. His dreams, like those of many Americans, centered upon the vast Spanish possessions to the west and south, temptingly rich lands that were weakly held by Spaniards who had blocked American attempts to push trade beyond the mountain frontiers, to the point of arousing demands for war against them.

Burr's grand schemes involved settlement and conquest of the Spanish lands, and perhaps he envisioned himself as an American Napoleon, an Emperor of a New America of the West who would lead his forces all the way to Mexico where he could crown his beloved daughter Theodosia as queen. Nobody ever was certain because Burr changed his story every time he whispered it to anybody who might lend him money or support.

Burr first apparently tried to swindle the British government. He knew that British Minister Anthony Merry was working to divide the Union and that some leading New England Federalists, siding with Britain, had been plotting secession from the United States. Even before his term as Vice-President ended, Burr secretly approached the British Minister with the startling proposal that if England backed him with enough money he might be able to separate the eastern states from the western states and build a new country in the Southwest.

Historians were never able to agree on whether Burr was serious about it or was just taking advantage of the widespread talk of secession both by New Englanders who feared the government was leading them to war with Britain and by dissatisfied westerners who thought the government should go to war with Spain. Burr's real desire was to promote money for his own schemes, and he seemed ready to promise almost anything to anybody if it would produce the necessary cash. British Minister Merry forwarded Burr's suggestion to London, but the British government did nothing about it, probably guessing Burr meant to put the money to his own purposes instead of theirs.

In the spring of 1805, Burr traveled into the West and began to gather a small following. He went down the Mississippi to New Orleans and back overland, telling various stories along the way. His talk of establishing American colonies of settlement in Spanish lands appealed to a wealthy Irish visionary, Harman Blennerhassett, who had settled in a mansion on an island in the Ohio River. Burr also gained the sympathy of some senators and representatives who were big land speculators, and of a young Nashville lawyer, Andrew Jackson, then commander of the Tennessee militia. Jackson was ready to sympathize with anyone who opposed Spanish rule in America, and as a duelist himself he thought Burr had suffered unfairly because of his duel with Hamilton.

In New Orleans crowds turned out to give a hero's reception to Burr as the man who might lead them against the Spaniards who occupied "American land." He was cordially received by the military commander of New Orleans, the highest ranking officer in the American Army, General James Wilkinson. Whatever Burr's plot was, and perhaps Burr never really was sure himself, Wilkinson soon became a key figure in it. Wilkinson, involved in devious plots of his own that called for treachery against the United States, thought he could use Burr to further his ambitions, and Burr thought that he could use Wilkinson.

At the time that Burr and Wilkinson began scheming together, although the fact would not be revealed for years to come, the ranking general of the Army had long been a paid spy for Spain. Wilkinson was playing a dangerous three-way secret agent game of trying to impress the American government with his patriotic loyalty, while serving the interests of Spain against the United States, and at the same time plotting with Burr against the Spanish.

To many Americans, especially in the West, there was nothing unpatriotic about Burr's activities against Spanish rule. President Jefferson had issued a public warning that unless the Spaniards quit interfering with American trade and kept their soldiers from violating American territory the result might be war. Congress was considering resolutions to declare that a state of hostilities already existed. But behind the open belligerence, Jefferson was carrying on peaceful negotiations with Spain to end the threat of war on the western frontier.

Burr had no knowledge of that. On Blennerhassett's Island in the Ohio River, he had begun collecting a small group of men and supplies for a mysterious voyage down the Mississippi. Whether it was merely a colonizing effort or a war party nobody knew.

General Wilkinson started to worry over the publicity Burr was getting and decided to turn the situation to his own advantage by betraying Burr as a traitor and pretending he had gone along with the scheme only to find out what Burr was up to. The general saw a double gain for himself in making a show of loyalty to the United States and secretly reassuring Spain that he was looking out for its interests as a well-paid spy should.

One of Burr's followers, Samuel Swartwout of New York, had carried a coded message overland to Wilkinson in New Orleans. Another of Burr's confidential agents, Justus Bollman, had come to New Orleans by sea with a similar ciphered message. General Wilkinson, after thinking it over for a few weeks, sent President Jefferson what he said was a true summary of Burr's plans. The double-dealing general's highly colored version pictured New Orleans as being in great peril and himself as its brave defender who meant to save the city and the nation from a traitorous plot. At the same time he secretly sent assurances of his loyalty as a spy to the Spanish Viceroy in Mexico.

Jefferson, who deeply mistrusted Burr, feared he might lead the hotheaded frontiersmen to start a war on their own and upset the delicate negotiations with Spain. He called his Cabinet into session, read them Wilkinson's letter, and then issued a proclamation warning that unnamed individuals were engaged in a conspiracy against Spain and calling upon them to cease their activities. Jefferson left Burr's name out of it for the time being and gave no hint that there might be treason involved or any plot to divide the Union.

When the Presidential proclamation reached Ohio the local militia decided to raid Blennerhassett's Island and capture Burr's "army" that supposedly was forming there. Actually the "army" was only a group of a few dozen young men. They escaped down the river during the night, leaving the raiders nothing much to capture but a supply of liquor in Blennerhassett's mansion, which they consumed while plundering and wrecking the house.

General Wilkinson, meanwhile, was firing up public passion in New Orleans, where he warned the citizens that a great horde of outlaws bent upon capturing the city was about to descend upon them. To meet the "emergency," he began rounding up "dangerous men," most of them dangerous only to himself, and throwing them into jail. As Army commander, he defied the courts, ignored writs of *habeas corpus,* and had Burr's messengers, Swartwout and Bollman, carried aboard a warship to be delivered to authorities in Washington along with what Wilkinson swore was an exact translation of Burr's coded letter. When an "advance flotilla" of Burr's forces came down the lower Mississippi, Wilkinson ordered the group arrested. Despite the mighty alarm, the "flotilla" turned out to be a group of boys on a few log rafts.

Burr, unaware of all the hysteria over his activities, came down the Mississippi with another small group of men in nine boats. The Acting Governor of the Mississippi Territory, Cowles Mead, called out the militia and stopped him, but reported that fears had been greatly exaggerated. Once again, there was no massive armed force, but only what might have been a group of colonizers, "and the major part of these boys or young men just from school." Burr was seized, but quickly paroled. When he attempted to escape to Spanish territory, he was captured again, and was taken east by armed guard for trial.

In Washington, John Randolph was demanding in Congress that the people had a right to know what was behind the President's message warning of a conspiracy. Jefferson gave the House of Representatives his answer on January 22, 1807, sending with it part of the Wilkinson correspondence, including the cipher letter from Burr which had been decoded to read that "the gods invite us to glory and fortune." The President flatly denounced Burr as a traitor who had plotted to divide the United States and declared that there could be no question about his guilt.

Some Americans were not that sure. They suspected Jefferson of making a scapegoat of Burr for political reasons and personal revenge. While the whole country was excited over the sensational charges, Bollman and Swartwout were brought to Washington and confined to military barracks. Jefferson's Senate leader, William Giles, immediately proposed an emergency measure to keep the two "dangerous criminals" in prison pending trial by suspending the writ of *habeas corpus*. The Senate, in secret session, rushed through a bill and asked the House to concur as promptly and secretly.

But the House explosively refused to act in secret and decided on free and open debate. Members strongly protested that the suspension of writs of *habeas corpus* by the British back in the days when a king ruled the colonies had been one of the reasons Americans fought for independence. Personal liberty became the battle cry of Congress and the House voted down the bill for suspension of *habeas corpus* 113 to 19.

That left the Burr conspiracy to the courts. The case first came before Chief Justice Marshall and the Supreme Court early in February, 1807, in the form of an appeal by Bollman and Swartwout from a ruling by a District of Columbia court that they should be held as prisoners without bail.

Hearing it as almost his first case was another new member of the Court that term, a distinguished New Yorker, Brockholst Livingston, appointed by President Jefferson to fill a vacancy caused by the death the previous September of Justice Paterson. Livingston, a vigorous-minded man with independent views, proved to be no rubber stamp for the Jeffersonians. There were times when he differed with Marshall, but on basic constitutional issues Livingston was with him.

The case of *Ex Parte Bollman* presented the Court with its first chance to interpret what the drafters of the Constitution meant when they carefully defined treason. Under the laws of England and other Old World nations, those in power often used charges of treason to get rid of political opponents, and judges loosely applied the word "treason" to almost any act that would provide an excuse. It was to protect American citizens against such politically inspired charges that the framers of the Constitution strictly limited and defined the crime by declaring:

"Treason against the United States shall consist only in levying war against them, or in adhering to their enemies, giving them aid and comfort. No person shall be convicted of treason unless on the testimony of two witnesses to the same overt act, or on confession in open court."

The Constitution promised that, on those specific terms, even a dangerous and unpopular citizen was entitled to have his rights protected from mass hysteria and the enmity of those in power. It was a promise that now was to be put to the test.

The evidence put before the Court, in addition to the letters and an affidavit from Wilkinson, included a new accusation by a man who had become an American hero, General William Eaton. During the troubles with the pirates of the Barbary States of North Africa, Eaton had gathered together a small band of men and staged an heroic overland march from Egypt to take Tripoli from the rear, capturing the seaport of Derna. Wildly acclaimed for his military feat, he became the hero of the day on his return to the United States, but the government was slow in paying his expenses.

Suddenly President Jefferson put pressure on Congress to settle Eaton's long overdue claims. Three days later, Eaton signed an affidavit that Burr once had tried to lure him into what he said was a plan to overthrow the United States government with the aid of dissatisfied Naval officers. It was a plan which supposedly included dark talk of assassinating Jefferson, doing away with Congress, and seizing the government by force.

Eaton said that at the time he first learned about it he had suggested Jefferson should appoint Burr to some foreign mission to get him out of the country before he made trouble. But Eaton never did explain satisfactorily why he failed to tell the President the details until he was anxious to be paid for his North African mission.

The opinion Marshall read for the majority of the Court was a definitive statement of the American law of treason. He held that acts of conspiracy less than war, no matter how atrocious, were not treason within the strict limits of the Constitution. That did not mean that such crimes as plotting against the government should go unpunished, he said, but the Constitution had rightly left it up to Congress to pass whatever laws might be necessary to deal with "crimes that have not ripened into treason."

The framers of the Constitution had not only defined and limited treason to a witnessed or confessed assembly of men for an open act of war, but had been jealous in protecting that limitation. "It is therefore more safe as well as more consonant with the principles of our Constitution that the crime of treason should not be extended by construction to doubtful cases," he said, "and that crimes not clearly within the constitutional definition should receive such punishment as the legislature in its wisdom may provide." He held that: "To constitute that specific crime for which the prisoners now before the Court have been committed, war must be actually levied against the United States."

Marshall decided that Eaton's affidavit, whatever it might prove about Burr, did not specifically involve Bollman and Swartwout. Wilkinson's affidavit and Burr's coded letter might indicate various conspiracies but they were not evidence that the two messengers were part of an actual gathering of men to make war against the United States. "Therefore, as the crime with which the prisoners stand charged has not been committed," Marshall said, "the Court can only direct them to be discharged."

Republicans were furious that Bollman and Swartwout had been set free, because it reflected upon Jefferson's motives in accusing Burr of treason. Some of Jefferson's supporters renewed the clamor that Marshall should be impeached, but after the Chase trial nobody really took such threats seriously. A Supreme Court Justice couldn't be impeached for the opinions he handed down. There was also excited talk of trying to change the law so as to deprive the Supreme Court of jurisdiction over all criminal cases, but it came to nothing.

Even if such a law were passed, Marshall would be the judge of Aaron Burr. The case before the Supreme Court in Washington was only a preliminary. Burr was being brought as a prisoner to the court in Richmond, where Marshall would sit as a circuit judge.

In the Virginia that was both Marshall's state and Jefferson's, their long political enmity would be the background for the trial of the former Vice-President of the United States as a traitor. Some would see nothing but malice in the zeal with which Jefferson pursued Burr. Jefferson put all the power of the Presidency, his personal influence and that of his party, and the liberal use of public funds into the effort, and devoted hours of his own time to collecting evidence and directing the prosecution. Others would accuse Marshall of using his position as a judge to prevent Burr's conviction, mainly because he knew Jefferson hated Burr and wanted him convicted. But such charges against both Jefferson and Marshall were made by excited partisans.

Jefferson, whatever his political goals, was genuinely convinced Burr was guilty. Like the slain Hamilton, he had come to fear the dapper little genius of plots and intrigues and he sincerely believed Burr was a menace to society. Marshall, whatever his Federalist sympathies for a man persecuted by the Republicans for political reasons, was genuinely interested in seeing to it that Burr was fairly treated under the Constitution and that his rights were fully protected. Both did what they thought best for the nation.

B Y THE time John Marshall arrived home from Washington the end of March, 1807, Richmond was overcrowded with important visitors, journalists and mobs of the just plain curious, drawn by what was to be the seven-month trial of Aaron Burr. It was what Marshall called "the most unpleasant case ever to be brought before a judge in this and perhaps any other country."

The prisoner was waiting for him under military guard, and he was a sorry sight, still dressed in the shabby suit and battered white hat he had been wearing when he was captured. Burr had been made to live and to sleep in those clothes during one thousand miles of forced travel from the Mississippi wilderness to Virginia, over Indian trails, through swamps and rainstorms, surrounded by soldiers and protesting all the way against his military arrest and the denial of his right to a hearing before a civilian court.

Marshall immediately signed an order transferring him to the custody of civil authorities and Burr was temporarily confined to a room in the Eagle Tavern. Preliminary hearings were held there, then moved to the courtroom at the capitol, and when that wasn't large enough to hold the clamoring mob of spectators, court finally was shifted to the big hall of the Virginia House of Delegates where the rest of the trial was held.

United States District Attorney George Hay moved to commit Burr to jail without bail to await trial on charges of treason and misdemeanor, declaring that at the time of his capture Burr was on his way to attack Mexico and that he intended to seize New Orleans and "make it the capital of his empire." Defense attorney John Wickham argued that Burr had been acting patriotically since nearly everybody expected war with Spain, and that in the event there was no war Burr would have turned his expedition to the peaceful enterprise of "settlements beyond the Mississippi." Burr also spoke for himself, claiming he was being persecuted "on mere conjecture," and that the whole country had been unjustly aroused against him because Wilkinson had frightened the President and Jefferson had falsely alarmed the people.

Marshall refused to hold Burr without bail on a charge of treason, since the government as yet had produced no evidence of that, but did agree to hold him for "high misdemeanor," which would permit his temporary release on bail. Hay wanted bail set at one hundred thousand dollars, but Marshall decided ten thousand dollars would be "about right." Bond money was raised by a group of Burr's wealthy Richmond sympathizers.

In ruling on the question of admitting Burr to bail, Marshall had spoken of the "hand of malignity" that "may grasp any individual against whom its hate may be directed or whom it may capriciously seize," and many took that to be a direct criticism of President Jefferson. But Marshall told reporters during a court recess that he had not meant to reflect upon the President in any way.

Jefferson, personally directing the prosecution through the government attorneys, knew that much of his political popularity would rest on the outcome of the case. Three months before, in his special message to Congress, he had flatly declared that Burr was guilty "beyond question." Now he complained in letters that the public mind was being filled with "anxiety and doubt" and that he wasn't sure "what will be proved" against Burr, but that he had "set on foot an inquiry through the whole of the country" that should produce witnesses who would "satisfy the world if not the judges" of Burr's treason.

In Washington, cabinet meetings were held to put every resource of the government behind the case, and Secretary of State Madison was told to spare no expense in bringing witnesses to Richmond. A dragnet was spread over the country to discover every possible witness and justices of the peace were directed to examine anybody who might have the slightest knowledge of Burr's plans, movements or conversations.

Among the reporters covering the trial was a young New Yorker, Washington Irving. Andrew Jackson also was in Richmond, defying the popular passion against Burr by delivering street-corner speeches praising him as a brave patriot who would have led Americans against the hated Spanish. Burr's daughter Theodosia soon arrived to comfort her father and charm his friends, and the waiting witnesses included General Eaton, hero of the African campaign against the Barbary pirates, who swaggered about Richmond in colorful Egyptian garb and was obviously delighted to be asked for his autograph.

On May 22, Marshall took his place on the bench again, with District Court Judge Cyrus Griffin beside him to do little more than nod his assent to whatever Marshall decided, and the next step in the trial began. A grand jury was to decide whether or not to indict Burr for treason, but there was a preliminary skirmish over the seating of the jury.

Burr personally challenged the seating of two of his worst political enemies—Senator William Nicholas, who admitted he would be happy to see Burr shot as a traitor, and William Giles, Jefferson's Senate leader. They were replaced, and one of the places was taken by John Randolph, Jefferson's former leader of the House, who had become his firm enemy. Randolph was named foreman of the grand jury, which finally included fourteen Republicans, several of them Jefferson's close friends, and only two Federalists.

District Attorney Hay then moved again to have Burr jailed without bail on the charge of treason because Wilkinson, the government's main witness against him, had not yet arrived and he feared Burr might try to escape before Wilkinson got there. Marshall decided it was the court's duty to hear the motion, but he criticized Hay for making it in a manner that might influence the jury before testimony was heard.

Marshall said he deplored "any attempt . . . to prejudice the public judgment and to try any person" not by the law and the evidence but "by public feelings which may be and often are artificially excited against the innocent as well as the guilty." After more wrangling, attorneys for both sides agreed Burr temporarily should remain at liberty by furnishing additional bail.

While everybody was waiting for Wilkinson to show up, Jefferson suggested in instructions to Hay that the trial might provide good publicity for an attack on Marshall's previous opinion in the *Marbury vs. Madison* case. "I have long wished for a proper occasion to have the gratuitous opinion in *Marbury vs. Madison* brought before the public and denounced as not law," he wrote. Jefferson cautioned Hay, however, not to involve him personally in the trial.

Burr made an attempt to do just that. He presented a motion to subpoena President Jefferson in person as a witness, to force him to produce certain papers in court that Burr claimed were orders to the Army and Navy to "destroy his person and properties." Marshall called for arguments on the motion and by then Luther Martin had arrived to join Burr's defense staff. Martin charged that if Jefferson refused to become a witness he would be "substantially a murderer." Martin accused the President of open prejudice in pursuing a fallen rival and turning upon Burr "the dogs of war, the hell-hounds of persecution," because of "anger, jealousy and hatred." Government attorneys answered as heatedly that it was Burr who was trying to arouse prejudice and "abuse the government."

Marshall appealed for reason and took both sides to task for making improper statements in the heat of debate. He advised counsel to "confine themselves on every occasion to the point really before the court." After several days of argument, Marshall ruled that there was nothing in the Constitution to exempt a President from being summoned as a witness, but that the President might decide his official duties prevented him from obeying such a summons. Nevertheless, the court had to issue it, however reluctantly, because "if it be a duty, the court can have no choice." Therefore he ordered a subpoena served on President Jefferson.

Jefferson wisely ignored it, but did agree to submit voluntarily whatever papers the court might require, "reserving the necessary right of the President . . . to decide independently of all other authority what papers coming to him as President the public interest permits to be communicated." He pointed out in a letter to Hay that a President could not allow himself to become subject to commands of the courts which might "bandy him from pillar to post, keep him constantly trudging from north to south and east to west, and withdraw him entirely from his constitutional duties."

Wilkinson finally showed up in Richmond in mid-June. Resplendently attired in the full-dress uniform of the Commanding General of the Armies of the United States, he made a one-man parade through the crowded streets to the courtroom. Reporter Washington Irving wrote that Wilkinson "strutted into the court" and that as he was sworn in as a witness he "stood swelling like a turkey cock." But after he had spent four days on the witness stand, Wilkinson was thoroughly shaken. Sweating and ill at ease, he was forced to admit that in sending Burr's coded letter to Jefferson he had left out the first sentence which clearly showed that Burr had written in answer to a letter Wilkinson had sent him. The general also admitted that he had erased some of the words of Burr's letter and substituted others.

Before the grand jury got through with him, Wilkinson was almost indicted himself. Complaining indignantly that nobody had a right to call him a liar and a cheat, he escaped indictment by a narrow margin of two votes. The jury's foreman, John Randolph, confided to a friend that in his opinion "Wilkinson is the only man I ever saw who was from the bark to the very core a villain."

General Eaton took the stand to repeat his story that Burr had tried to get him to join in a plot to overthrow the government. Other witnesses also testified to having heard through third persons that Burr intimated intentions of dividing the Union. There was indirect testimony that Burr had tried to get soldiers to desert the Army and join his expedition. Two Navy men, Commodores Stephen Decatur and Thomas Truxtun, admitted that Burr had approached them about his plans, but said he had mentioned nothing about overthrowing the government.

Through all the testimony and arguments, Marshall was patient, careful in his rulings, and determined to let everybody have his full say. He also took pains to keep the constitutional definition of treason before the grand jury. According to law, as he kept pointing out, there had to be a proven overt act of war against the United States.

After some fifty witnesses had testified about Burr's expedition, the grand jury indicted Burr and Blennerhassett on both charges of treason and misdemeanor. The indictment placed the actual act of war as the gathering of Burr's followers on Blennerhassett's Island in the Ohio River, then part of Wood County, Virginia, on December 13, 1806. That was when the local militia had tried to capture the boys who escaped down the river and left them only Blennerhassett's mansion to plunder. The second charge of misdemeanor was that at the same time and place Burr and Blennerhassett had launched a military force against Spain, a country officially friendly to the United States.

The indictment ended Burr's freedom on bail. Marshall first permitted him to be kept under arrest in a barred and guarded but comfortable room at his attorney's home, but later ordered his removal to a three-room suite on the top floor of the state penitentiary. After setting August third as the date for the trial itself, Marshall took a brief and much-needed vacation at Oak Hill with Polly. Bitterness over the case had divided Richmond society and the personal attacks against Marshall so upset Polly that she suffered another nervous breakdown, one of the most severe of her life.

Soon forced back to the bench, Marshall supervised the tedious process of selecting a jury, which took two weeks since there was hardly a prospective juror who had not made up his mind in advance that Burr was a traitor, but twelve finally were accepted for the lack of more impartial citizens. There was little fresh evidence at the trial, but lawyers for both sides argued over it almost endlessly, and after listening all day Marshall spent many hot summer nights writing opinions on various points in dispute. Each morning he would make his rulings on the previous day's arguments, and some of his opinions ran almost as long as the speeches the lawyers had made.

General Eaton, as the government's first witness, was promptly challenged by Burr's attorneys on the grounds that an act of war had to be established before there could be testimony as to Burr's character and motives. But Marshall ruled that the government could conduct its case as it pleased, as long as Eaton confined himself to the crime charged in the indictment, the levying of war at Blennerhassett's Island. When Eaton took the stand again, he finally admitted: "Concerning any overt act which goes to prove Aaron Burr guilty of treason I know nothing, but concerning Burr's expressions of treasonable intentions, I know much."

The government then tried to establish an actual act of war, by putting some of Blennerhassett's workmen on the stand. One quoted him as saying it would be a good thing to divide the Union. Another said Blennerhassett had told him an expedition was going to Mexico where Burr would be emperor and his daughter queen. Secessionist newspaper articles were introduced and attempts were made to show the purchase of arms, food and boats. There was testimony that Burr, on his way to Blennerhassett's Island, had told friends that the western states were ready to split off from the Union and that it would take only a small force of husky young men to bring about the break. But other witnesses testified that what they had seen on the island itself seemed peaceful enough—men warming themselves at a fire, a few cleaning what might have been hunting rifles, but no real evidences of war.

With more than one hundred government witnesses still remaining to be heard, Burr's lawyers objected that there had been no proof of levying war against the United States and therefore it was improper to hear further testimony about something that had not happened. Lawyers debated the point for ten days. Marshall let them argue it out and then took a week end to write what was to be his most important opinion in the case. He read it on the last day of August to a hushed audience jammed into the House of Delegates.

It was a long opinion, fifty closely printed pages, and some of its minor passages were confusing, but it established constitutional limits of treason that were to guide future generations. Along with his previous opinion in the case of Bollman and Swartwout, it provided a bulwark of defense for the citizen against being charged with treason for political reasons.

Marshall held, in effect, that government prosecutors could not get around the plain constitutional provision that they must produce at least two witnesses to an actual act of levying war against the United States. To prove treason, the government would have to prove the act of war and then prove the individual's part in that act. The government could not rely in times of crisis on previously vague concepts of treason, but could, if it wished, adopt special laws against espionage and riot.

He decided Burr had not been "legally present" during the incident at Blennerhassett's Island upon which the charge of treason was based, that conspiring or plotting treason "is not treason in itself," and that the court was not satisfied there had been evidence of a gathering "in a condition to make war" rather than just a "secret fugitive assemblage." Since the government had admitted that none of its remaining witnesses could add anything to prove that Burr and Blennerhassett actually had levied war against the United States, Marshall held that further testimony as to other alleged crimes would be irrelevant. He told the jury it had before it all the evidence on the main point and that it was up to the jury to determine whether the defendants were guilty on that basis.

During the arguments, government attorneys had hinted strongly that if Marshall ruled against them he might yet be impeached, or that Congress might amend the Constitution to deprive the Court of some of its independence. In answer to such threats, Marshall commented in his opinion, "That this Court dares not usurp power is most true," but "that this Court dares not shrink from its duty is not less true." He said:

"No man is desirous of placing himself in a disagreeable

situation. No man is desirous of becoming the peculiar subject of calumny. No man, might he let the bitter cup pass from him without self-reproach, would drain it to the bottom. But if he has no choice in the case; if there is no alternative presented to him but a dereliction of duty, or the opprobrium of those who are denominated the world, he merits the contempt as well as the indignation of his country, who can hesitate which to embrace."

The next morning, after being out only a short time, the jury brought in a verdict of acquittal. It was worded, "not proved to be guilty under this indictment by any evidence submitted to us," and Burr's attorneys objected to that wording as a reflection upon the Court, but if it was meant to be a criticism Marshall ignored it. He ruled that the jury's words should be left on the bill of indictment, but that the record should show the customary simple verdict, "not guilty."

Still to be decided was the charge of misdemeanor, involving Burr's intentions toward Spanish territory, and that took another six weeks of trial. Furious that Burr had been cleared of treason, Jefferson sent fresh instructions to the government attorneys to press the misdemeanor charge. Jefferson, to the end of his life, believed Marshall had conspired to prevent the real evidence against Burr from being presented to the public.

But even on the charges of setting afoot a military expedition against Spanish territory, the government's case against Burr failed. Attempts then were made to bring still other charges, but with the main questions settled Marshall left Richmond for a rest in the mountains.

He left behind him an uproar. There were public demonstrations in many cities. Crowds in Baltimore and elsewhere hanged straw dummies of Marshall, Burr, Blennerhassett and Luther Martin. Republican newspapers denounced Marshall as a man who would forever "blot the fair page of American history." Jefferson sent Congress a special message, along with a copy of the Burr proceedings, asking for an investigation.

Burr slipped away to exile and poverty, to the tragedy of his daughter's drowning at sea, and to an old age of obscurity, deserted by all but a few faithful friends. Excitement over his trial might have lasted longer except for an overshadowing threat of war that diverted public attention. Jefferson, troubled with a decided loss of popularity, devoted himself to trying to prevent war with England, and Chief Justice Marshall went back to minding his Supreme Court.

⇛ CHAPTER ⇚

16

CHIEF JUSTICE MARSHALL took two hours out from hearings of an important case before the Supreme Court on Saturday, March 4, 1809, to administer the oath of office to a new President. He adjourned Court and went upstairs in the Capitol to the Chamber of the House of Representatives for the inauguration of James Madison, chosen by Jefferson as his successor and inheritor of the troubles that were sweeping America toward war with England.

Physically, Marshall towered above little Madison, and he also held a somewhat lower opinion of him than he had in the days when they were teamed to fight for the ratification of the Constitution. Marshall was delighted that Jefferson was no longer President, but he wondered if Madison would be enough of a statesman and active political leader to keep America out of Europe's war.

At the moment, however, Marshall was more interested in the case before the Court and after the brief inaugural ceremony he went back downstairs to continue the hearings. He had been somewhat reluctant to have the Court take the case at all since many believed it had been made up just to get the Court's judgment on the issues involved. Before the afternoon ended, attorneys asked to change some of their pleadings and Marshall agreed to that, so final arguments were put off for a year.

The suit of *Fletcher vs. Peck* was an outgrowth of the biggest land fraud in the nation's history. Fourteen years before, the state of Georgia had sold nearly all the western lands that later were to make up the states of Alabama and Mississippi to four companies of land speculators. The speculators bought the votes of members of the legislature with cash bribes and shares of stock and put through a deal that gave them more than thirty-five million acres of fertile, well-watered, heavily timbered land for less than one and one-half cents an acre. Called the Yazoo lands because of a river of that name that ran through part of the territory, they had suddenly become an even far richer prize for the speculators because Eli Whitney's invention of the cotton gin promised to make the area the best cotton land in the world.

Settlers began pouring into what had been wasteland and Georgia's citizens rose in rage when they realized the corrupt state government had practically given away what had become a treasure. Crowds marched on the capital and threatened to lynch the legislators, angry demonstrations spread over the state, repeal conventions were held, and the people "threw the rascals out" by electing a new legislature the next year. The reform legislature passed a bill declaring the land deals "null and void" because of the "atrocious speculation, corruption and collusion by which the usurped act and grants were obtained." Georgia reclaimed the land, annulled the whole transaction, and in a ceremony on the capitol steps the repealers publicly burned all records of the grant.

But the speculators had already spread out over the country selling parcels of land to purchasers in other states. Agents scattered thousands of pamphlets through the Middle States and New England, describing the Yazoo country as a paradise of rich land, mild and healthful climate and profitable investment. Throngs of buyers stormed the promoters' offices, some with cash in hand but most of them anxious to sign up for easy-payment plans that were offered. There was excited buying, selling and trading as almost everybody with a little money or credit tried to get in on the speculation. Bankers and groups of investors bought up the notes and large tracts of land.

Then the news came that Georgia had rescinded the grants and the boom collapsed, leaving thousands of purchasers holding apparently worthless notes and deeds. Some were financially ruined. As it turned out, Georgia had no right to sell much of the land in the first place, since it was Indian land protected by Federal treaties. Law suits were started and appeals were made to Congress.

Congress got Georgia to agree to turn over its western land to the Federal government in order to avoid the tangle of law suits as well as trouble with the Indians, in return for which five million acres would be set aside to cover claims against the state. A commission recommended that the reserved lands be sold so the money could be distributed to those who had been victimized. Among the strongest backers of the move were a group of New Englanders who had bought an interest in the four original and now propertyless speculating companies.

They formed a lobby to push the settlement through Congress, but their efforts were blocked for a time and Congress refused to act. In an attempt to prod Congress into action, the New England lobbyists designed an ingenious test case between two so-called "innocent purchasers" that would challenge Georgia's right to rescind the land grants. Since Georgia no longer held the land, having already transferred it to the Federal government, a Court decision could really change nothing. But it would give the lobbyists a strong argument if they could convince Congress they had the Constitution on their side.

John Peck of Boston, a dealer in the Georgia lands, sold or pretended to sell fifteen thousand acres to Robert Fletcher of Amherst. Fletcher then brought suit against Peck to recover the money, and lawyers wrote up the suit so it would cover every point of the dispute and present the main question of whether Georgia had a right to wipe out its grant of the land. The case dragged through the courts until it finally reached the Supreme Court.

At the first hearings in March, 1809, Luther Martin was Fletcher's lawyer and John Quincy Adams argued the case for Peck. When the Court heard the final arguments a year later, Adams' place was taken by another lawyer, Joseph Story, a young Bostonian who soon would become one of Marshall's Associate Justices and his closest friend.

It was pretty obvious that both sides wanted Peck to win and Martin's plea for Fletcher was deliberately a losing one. It was a loose and rambling oration on the corruption involved in the original Yazoo grant. Story based his case for Peck on the provision in the Constitution against impairing the obligation of a contract.

Story argued that Georgia had a right to sell the land and in doing so had made a contract which could not be cancelled simply because a different group of legislators later wanted to take back what had been sold. He told the Court that grants of land couldn't be voided by belated discoveries that members of the legislature had been bribed. "The parties now before the Court are innocent of the fraud, if any has been practiced," he said. "They were bona fide purchasers, for a valuable consideration, without notice of fraud. They cannot be affected by it."

Marshall delivered his opinion for the majority of the Court on March 16, 1810, and in doing so laid another foundation stone in the structure of American constitutional law. As in *Marbury vs. Madison,* he again strengthened the supremacy of the Court. He set precedent by declaring a state law unconstitutional and by extending protection of the Constitution to property rights. The decision had effects that reached far beyond the controversy over the Yazoo lands in setting down a law of public contract that helped stabilize American business and encourage the nation's commercial growth.

He held in the case of *Fletcher vs. Peck* that the rescinding act of the Georgia legislature was null and void because it violated the contract clause of the Constitution which said that "no state shall pass any . . . law impairing the obligation of contracts." Georgia, he held, was not an independent sovereign power but "a member of the American Union; and that Union has a Constitution, the supremacy of which all acknowledge, and which imposes limits to the legislatures of the several states, which none claim a right to pass." Since "a contract executed . . . differs in nothing from a grant," a state had no right to break a contract it had made.

Marshall decided that the Court could not examine the motives of legislators in passing a law, and that innocent purchasers would suffer if land grants could be upset on the grounds of corruption. That part of his opinion was based more on moral than legal argument. When a purchaser of land "has paid his money for a title good at law, he is innocent, whatever may be the guilt of others, and equity will not subject him to the penalties attached to that guilt," he said. "All titles would be insecure, and the intercourse between man and man would be very seriously obstructed if this principle be overturned."

He ruled, in effect, that a state had no more right to break a contract it had made than a private individual would have to break a contract with another individual. "The past cannot be recalled by the most absolute power," he said, and "a fact cannot cease to be a fact" because a state seeks to undo what has been done. "When, then, a law is in its nature a contract, where absolute rights have vested under that contract, a repeal of the law cannot divest those rights."

Critics said that in putting land grants under the Constitution's clause to protect contracts Marshall went beyond anything the framers of the Constitution intended. They also said he abandoned the tradition of common law which had long recognized fraud as a ground for annulment of contracts. His opinion was highly unpopular at the time because it seemed to many people to condone the Yazoo fraud, to strengthen doubtful land speculation, and to furnish the basis for questionable public land grants in the future. But he steadied the nation's commerce, checked a flood of contract-breaking laws, and tightened the ties of Federal government. More important, he gave to property rights some of the same protection the Constitution already had given to personal liberties.

The opinion had little direct effect on the Yazoo claims except for its influence in Congressional lobbying. Finally, four years later, the New Englanders and other "innocent purchasers" did get back some of their money when Congress appropriated nearly five million dollars to compensate them.

Six months after Marshall had delivered his *Fletcher vs. Peck* opinion, Justice William Cushing died, in September, 1810. That left only three old Federalists on the Supreme Court bench, Marshall, Bushrod Washington, and Samuel Chase. President Madison was certain to name a Republican to fill the vacancy, which meant that Republicans would be in the majority for the first time since the Supreme Court was organized.

But to former President Jefferson, that wasn't enough. "It will be difficult to find a character of firmness enough to preserve his independence on the same bench with Marshall," Jefferson wrote Madison. He considered "old Cushing's" death a "fortunate" event which would give Republicans their chance to reform the Court, but said no "milk-and-water associate" would do. To stand up to what Jefferson called Marshall's "twistifications of the law," a man of "unquestionable Republican principles" was needed.

The Court had been enlarged to seven members before Jefferson left office, mostly to provide another judge who could ride a new circuit in far-off Kentucky, Tennessee and Ohio. But that also had added one more Republican to the bench. Jefferson had appointed Thomas Todd, who had headed Kentucky's Court of Appeals. Cushing's death now would give the Republicans four Justices to outbalance Marshall, Washington and Chase. Jefferson began bombarding President Madison with "suggestions" and Madison did his best to follow them.

Jefferson's first recommendation was his former Attorney General, Levi Lincoln. Madison promptly offered the place to Lincoln but he declined because of approaching blindness. Connecticut's Republican boss, Alexander Wolcott, was then nominated, but he was such a flagrant political hack the Senate rejected him even though the Senate was overwhelmingly Republican. The new Justice had to come from New England because that had been Cushing's circuit, so Madison next appointed John Quincy Adams, who had deserted the Federalists to side with the Republicans and was then Minister to Russia. His appointment was confirmed but Adams declined to accept, preferring his diplomatic post.

Last on Jefferson's list was Boston lawyer Joseph Story. In writing to Madison, Jefferson had dismissed Story as "too young" and "unquestionably a tory." But Story was a Republican and Madison had run out of possibilities, so Story was made an Associate Justice of the Supreme Court at the age of thirty-two.

Meanwhile the balance of the Court suffered another upset. While Madison was searching for Cushing's successor, Justice

Chase died, leaving two vacancies instead of one. Madison had less trouble filling Chase's place and nominated Comptroller of the Treasury Gabriel Duval. The nominations of Story and Duval were confirmed at the same time, in November, 1811. Once again the seven-man Court was complete, and seemingly completely Republican except for Marshall and Bushrod Washington.

But it became more than ever "Marshall's Court." He continued to dominate it as fully as when its members had shared his own political faith. And Story became Marshall's ideal colleague, a man who in opposite habits and temperament so perfectly complemented Marshall's personality that they would be spoken of as "two sides of one man." Story enriched Marshall and Marshall steadied Story. In their affection and admiration for each other that grew through a quarter of a century, they were almost like father and son.

Handsome, impressionable, eager, with a voracious appetite for reading and with a mind that was an orderly storehouse of assorted knowledge, Story was a highly intellectual Harvard graduate. One of eighteen children of a wealthy family of Massachusetts' patriots, shipowners and merchants, he was, as his father had been, one of the few New Englanders of wealth and high social position who "dared avow themselves Republicans." An admirer of Jefferson and a supporter of Madison, he rose rapidly in Republican politics, but also won the approval of Federalist leaders for his "independent principles."

Story first became acquainted with Marshall in Washington as an attorney before Congress and the Supreme Court. During the Georgia land controversy case he took most of his meals at the same boarding house as members of the Court and the friendship grew. "I love his laugh," Story wrote a friend about Marshall. "It is too hearty for an intriguer—and his good temper and unwearied patience are equally agreeable on the bench and in the study." Later, he impulsively wrote, "I am in love with his character, positively in love."

From the time Story took his place on the bench, he came under the spell of Marshall's personality and although they sometimes disagreed, and quite strongly, they shared not only their work but the deepest personal confidence in each other. Over the years their relationship became so trusting they freely exchanged sympathetic advice on family problems, health, finances, and intimate details of their daily lives. They had friendly arguments over poetry, popular novels, theater, and favorite foods, shared in social activities when they were together in Washington, and wrote long and frequent letters when they were apart.

Story had a passion for research and for the toil of delving into details; Marshall's vision was broad, seeking to sift away details and strike to the heart of a problem with a comprehensive view of general principles. Marshall detested the labor of investigating legal authorities and Story delighted in it. When they were considering Court decisions it was said that Marshall would tell Story, "That, Story, is the law. Now you find the precedents."

Marshall's influence over the other Justices, if in lesser degree, was the same as that he had upon Story. The character and personality that had won him friends all his life became his strength in leading the Court. Accustomed to Richmond's convivial society and to the warm good fellowship of other men, he forced no opinions upon his fellow Justices, but in most cases they came to see things his way, usually without realizing they were being led.

There were few men as convincing as Marshall in face-to-face discussions or in the penetrating use of logic that could draw others, with what Story called "the inevitability of gradualness," to his own constitutional faith. Republicans they might be, and never simply props for Marshall's views, but they were also younger men who admired and respected him as head of the Court family.

In a real sense they were a "family" during the seven or eight weeks each year that Court was in session in Washington. With their wives left at home, they were temporary bachelors sharing the same boarding house in what Story called "the most frank and unaffected intimacy." As Story wrote a friend a year after his appointment, "We live very harmoniously and familiarly. Indeed, we are all united as one, with a mutual esteem which makes even the labors of jurisprudence light." Sitting around together after dinner, or gathered in Marshall's room, they informally talked over the day's arguments in Court, and by "familiar conferences at our lodgings often came to a very quick and . . . accurate opinion, in a few hours."

They lived together "as agreeably as absence from friends and families could make our residence" and their "social hours, when undisturbed with the labors of law," were "passed in gay and frank conversation." Joking about incidents in Court, about the habits and clothing of some of the more pompous lawyers who appeared before them, trading stories, news of the day, the gossip of Washington society, they were "perfectly unconstrained." Two of the Justices were widowers and "objects of considerable attraction among the ladies," and so the others had "fine sport at their expense" amusing themselves "with some touches at match-making."

The Justices also held a regular "consultation day" in a room at the Capitol to reach more formal decisions, but even there humor brightened their tasks. The consultations took all day and sometimes lasted into the night, with meals brought in while discussions went on. It was a rule that wine was not to be served except in wet weather, when a glass or two might be excused on the grounds that it would ward off colds.

But as Story told it, Marshall sometimes relaxed the rule. He would ask Story to "step to the window and see if it does not look like rain." If Story answered that the sun was shining brightly, Marshall might reply that "our jurisdiction extends over so large a territory that the doctrine of chance makes it certain that it must be raining somewhere," and upon that mock ruling the wine would be served.

Marshall shrank from personal publicity. He appreciated honors that came his way, election to membership in historical, philosophical and various learned societies, and the conferring of honorary degrees by Princeton, Harvard and other universities, but he shunned those who wanted to write articles in praise of him or who attempted to interview him about his life and character. He told a friend, "I hope they will let me alone until I am dead."

While he thoroughly enjoyed informal social gatherings, he heartily disliked the formal dinners and receptions of Washington society, some of which he felt forced to attend. After dining with the President and attending a series of diplomatic affairs, he wrote Polly, "I have been more in company than I wish. . . . I go to them with reluctance and am bad company while there. I hope we have seen the last, but I fear we must encounter one more."

In off-hours at his Washington boarding house he was as casual in manner as he was at home in Richmond. Once when a lawyer's son was brought to the house to be introduced to the Chief Justice, Marshall noticed how uneasy the boy was, seeming awe-stricken in the presence of the "great man." So he broke up the lofty conversation and challenged the youngster to a game of marbles. Marshall led him off into the back yard and soon was down on his knees in the dirt, hard at play with the boy, the adults forgotten.

On Court days he often arrived in the courtroom early and sat among the lawyers, talking and joking until he finally had to go and put on his robes over his usually rumpled and neglected clothing. When a young lawyer, new to practice, tried to flatter Marshall by remarking that the Chief Justice had reached "the acme of judicial distinction," Marshall broke in and said. "Let me tell you what that means, young man. The acme of judicial distinction means the ability to look a lawyer straight in the eyes for two hours and not hear a damned word he says."

But when time came for him to open Court he took his place on the bench with great dignity. Clad in his robes of office, with the Associate Justices on either side of him, he could suddenly appear as majestic as a king on the throne. Grave, firm, concentrating and intent, Marshall let nobody forget for a moment that this was the Supreme Court of the United States.

He took full advantage of the brilliant talent and learning of the noted lawyers who appeared before him, such men as Luther Martin, William Pinkney, Samuel Dexter, William Wirt, Jeremiah Mason, Joseph Hopkinson and Daniel Webster. Their oratory filled the courtroom with admiring spectators and Marshall encouraged extended arguments. No time limit was put on them and a single lawyer sometimes would speak for two or three days, providing a wealth of discussion that often helped Marshall and his fellow Justices form their opinions.

Marshall was grateful even to counsel whose views he rejected because they helped stimulate his powers of analysis. "He was solicitous to hear arguments and not to decide causes without hearing them," Story wrote. "And no judge ever profited more by them. No matter what the subject was, new or old . . . buried under a mass of obsolete learning, or developed for the first time yesterday—whatever its nature, he courted argument, nay demanded it."

As America was driven into war against England in June, 1812, by increasingly hostile British actions at sea, by Madison's bungling peace efforts, and even more by Henry Clay's war hawks of Congress and their super-patriotic vision of glorious military victory, Marshall firmly kept his resolve of holding himself and the Court aloof from the public passions of the time. But while he publicly maintained strict silence, he made it clear in private letters that he was against the war, against the war hawks, and unhappy with Madison's diplomatic failure to keep the peace.

His sympathies were all with the Federalists, who hoped to revive the party and defeat Madison for re-election that year on the peace issue. Some of them decided Marshall might make a good candidate for President, to draw together Federalist and neutral anti-war voters. A mild boom was started to put him into the race against Madison and it won the backing of some newspapers. But Marshall apparently didn't take it seriously, and in any event indicated no desire to leave the Supreme Court. He was far more interested in another project that took him out of the heat of the Presidential campaign.

He had been chosen by Virginia to head a commission that would explore the wilderness rivers and streams and determine the possibilities of using the waterways for steamboat transportation to serve the thousands of settlers who were taking up new lands beyond the mountains. So, at the age of fifty-seven, Marshall set out on an expedition that let him recapture something of the spirit of his frontier boyhood.

Tramping through forests, climbing mountains, traveling by canoe, horseback, and more often on foot, he supervised the careful surveying with chain and spirit level of a route from Lynchburg to the Ohio. Much of the course he laid out was used years later in building the Chesapeake and Ohio Railroad.

In his report in 1812 he predicted the West was about to grow "in wealth and population with a rapidity which baffles calculation" and that the "practice so entirely novel as the use of steam in navigation" promised enormous changes in "that mysterious future which is in reserve." But his conclusion was that while the proposed waterway was entirely possible, it probably would be too expensive in competition with other means of westward travel.

Marshall returned home from his explorations to find Madison re-elected and the war going badly. On March 4, 1813, he administered the oath of office to Madison for a second time, and the Court soon became overwhelmed with cases growing out of wartime problems that involved economic measures, captured ships, and lost cargoes. In the aftermath of the British capture of Washington in 1814 and the burning of public buildings, the Court was forced to find housing where it could, but with the coming of peace it returned to a small room in the North Wing of the Capitol, which was described as "little better than a dungeon."

The Federalist party was dead and the country had a brief period of one-party rule and an "Era of Good Feelings." Entering his vigorous sixties, Marshall was pleased in March, 1817, to officiate at the Presidential inauguration of his old schoolmate, James Monroe, a ceremony that for the first time was held outdoors on a platform at the east portico of the Capitol.

But the nation's "good feelings" were on the surface and beneath it was a turmoil of disunity. Forces were at work that were to threaten the whole concept of strong Federal government. Against them, Marshall became more than ever the nation-builder whose vision and courage gave enduring definition to the purposes of the Constitution.

⇒≫ CHAPTER ≪⇐

17

CHIEF JUSTICE MARSHALL delivered three important opinions during a single six-week term of the Supreme Court that began in February, 1819, and the last of the three probably had a greater effect upon national government than any other opinion he ever wrote.

When the Court arrived in Washington for the start of its term it found that its old quarters in the Capitol basement had been restored, redecorated and enlarged, but there still was an overflow of spectators who had to stand under the arches that held up the floor of the Senate. Marshall and the other Justices took their places on a raised platform, looking across at wall decorations that represented Fame, the Constitution, and Justice. From the sleeve of his robe, he pulled out an eighteen-page document he had been working on during a summer vacation with Polly in the Virginia mountains, and announced that the Court had reached a decision in the first case on the docket, that of *Dartmouth College vs. Woodward,* which had been argued at the previous term.

It was a decision that was to have enormous effect upon the growth of American business and industry. The case involved a long and bitter dispute over the operation of Dartmouth College that had drawn much of New England into a raging controversay over religion, politics, and educational freedom.

The little New Hampshire school, started by missionaries as a charity institution to educate and Christianize the Indians, was given a Royal charter in 1769 which granted a group of trustees and "their successors forever" the power to run it, appoint officers, and make rules and regulations. Half a century later, Dartmouth found itself without any Indians but in the center of a battle for control of its administration and teachings. Lined up on one side were Congregationalists and old guard Federalists, and on the other side Republicans and the rest of the Protestant sects.

When the state government went Republican in 1816 the legislature passed an act amending the college charter and increasing the number of trustees so as to take control away from the old trustees and convert the college into a state university. Those who previously had been in charge of the college refused to recognize the new trustees and for a time there were two Dartmouths operating separately. William Woodward, who had been the college secretary for years, went over to the newly created university, and took the charter and all the record books with him. The old trustees went to court and sued Woodward to get them back.

Their attorneys argued that the state law amending Dartmouth's charter violated the contract provision of the Constitution. But New Hampshire's Superior Court of Appeals decided that the state legislature had a right to amend the charter, on the grounds that the college was a public institution, not a private one, because it was devoted to the public purpose of education. The New Hampshire court held that the Constitution's contract clause was intended "to protect private rights only," and that a corporation charter was not a contract so the Constitution could not limit the power of the state.

Carried to the Supreme Court on an appeal, the case was argued during three days of March, 1818. Dartmouth's old trustees were represented by Joseph Hopkinson and by Daniel Webster, a loyal Dartmouth graduate, then only thirty-six but already winning fame as an orator. Webster had argued the case before the state court and he based his appeal on the same arguments, but devoted more time to emotional oratory than to the question of whether New Hampshire's legislature had violated the Constitution. He reportedly brought spectators to tears with his eloquent plea that state control would destroy not only Dartmouth but "every college and all the literary institutions of the country." Speaking directly to Marshall after the formal arguments had been completed, according to reports published later, Webster said:

"Sir, you may destroy this little institution; it is weak, it is in your hands. But if you do so, you must carry through your work. You must extinguish, one after another, all those great lights of science which, for more than a century, have thrown radiance over our land. Dartmouth is, Sir, as I have said, a small college. And yet, there are those who love it. . . ."

More to the legal point, Hopkinson argued that Dartmouth was a private institution and that its charter as such was a contract which New Hampshire had no right to impair. When the arguments ended, Marshall announced that since "some judges had not formed opinions," the case would be carried over to the next term. Guesses were that the Court was about evenly divided. Marshall went off to Virginia, wrote his opinion, consulted by mail with the other Justices, and again after he reached Washington, and by the time the Court began its new term he had a majority behind him.

The opinion he pulled from his sleeve and began reading at the start of the 1819 session got right to the point. He said:

"The single question now to be considered is, do the acts to which the verdict refers violate the Constitution of the United States?" His answer was that the acts of the New Hampshire legislature, amending Dartmouth's charter, did violate the Constitution because, as he put it almost curtly, "It can require no argument to prove that the circumstances of this case constitute a contract." The college was a private charity, he held, not a public institution but a private corporation. Then he gave what was to become an often quoted definition of a corporation:

"A corporation is an artificial being, invisible, intangible, and existing only in contemplation of the law. . . . It possesses only those properties which the charter of its creation confers upon it. . . . By these means, a perpetual succession of individuals are capable of acting for the promotion of the particular object, like one immortal being. . . ."

His broad interpretation read into the Constitution a meaning he was convinced it implied, not only because of what it said but because of what it avoided saying. While "the preservation of rights of this description was not particularly in the view of the framers of the Constitution when the clause under consideration was introduced into that instrument," he said, that did not mean the writers of the Constitution meant to make an exception to the general rule and therefore the Court had no right to make that exception. The contract clause was made part of the Constitution "to give stability to contracts" and its "plain import" was to include corporations.

If there were holes in his argument, Marshall bridged the gaps with soaring sweeps of logic and firm moral statement. His ruling prohibited the states from changing the terms of corporate charters in much the same way his *Fletcher vs. Peck* decision had protected land grants. He held, in effect, that once a state granted a charter to a corporation, it had to abide by whatever the terms of that charter were at the time it was granted.

Dartmouth gained the protection it wanted against state interference, but so did American business, which soon took far more advantage of the decision. Protected from state interference, the power of corporations was enormously expanded, and there was a scramble for charters as the full import of the decision became understood.

Shortly after the decision was announced, Justice Story wrote a friend, "Unless I am very much mistaken the principles on which the decision rests will be found to apply with an extensive reach to all the greatest concerns of the people. . . ." He was not mistaken. Within a year, the *North American Review* noted that "perhaps no judicial proceedings in this country ever involved more important consequences."

Industries and enterprises of all kinds began to take advantage of the new Constitutional protection. Turnpike, canal and bridge companies, and later the railroads, besieged legislatures for charters. The Court decision reassured investors in corporate securities, made corporation franchises far more valuable, and generally gave new confidence and stimulation to the business world. The "extensive reach" that Story foresaw helped nourish and support the American industrial revolution.

But on the bad side it also stimulated corporate greed and political bribery, the corruption of legislatures, abuses of power and selfish disregard for public interests. Gradually the implied doctrine that a state was powerless to control the corporations it created was modified. The Court itself tempered later rulings. Legislatures learned to insert clauses in the charters they granted that reserved the right to alter, amend or repeal them, and "police powers" were more broadly applied to regulate corporations.

Marshall's second important opinion of 1819 extended the

Constitution's protection of contracts and again helped establish the Supreme Court's right to review the laws of states that were in conflict with national law. Having ruled in previous decisions that states had no right to interfere with land grants or corporation charters, the Court turned to contracts "between man and man for the payment of money" in the case of *Sturges vs. Crowninshield*. It was an opinion that for a time made Marshall one of America's most hated men.

When the Court began its 1819 term, America was suffering from its first nationwide depression. Unscrupulous and uncontrolled banks, the collapse of the paper money system, wildcat speculation, and over-extended credit had brought on bankruptcies, the repudiation of debts and contracts, and financial chaos. Thousands of settlers lost farms, city people were out of work, commercial houses shut down, and industries closed their doors.

The newly revived Bank of the United States, after first expanding credit, clamped down on debtors and refused to accept any money in payment of debts except the currency it issued itself. This worked a heavy hardship on people who held paper money issued by various state banks.

Meanwhile the number of state banks multiplied into the hundreds and all of them began printing more and more paper money, which often had no assets behind it. Some of it was good one day and worthless the next, and some of the banks even refused to accept their own currency in payment of debts. A man might have thousands of dollars worth of paper money printed by some bank and owe that bank a debt of only a few hundred dollars but still lose his property because the bank refused to take its own money in payment.

Banks and bankers became the villains of America and the Bank of the United States was hated the most. People who found their dollar bills turning into worthless scraps of paper, and those suffering from other hardships of depression, cried out to their state legislatures for relief. Some states refused charters to the Bank of the United States to keep it from opening branches and others passed laws to try to tax its branches out of business.

Many states started passing bankruptcy and insolvency laws to allow citizens to escape payment of debts. Honest citizens who were caught in the crisis and who were unable to pay took advantage of the laws, but so did swindlers who made use of the bankruptcy laws to pay off only a few dollars of their debts while they continued to live in luxury after declaring themselves bankrupt.

Marshall looked upon the entire situation with dismay. It reminded him of the utter financial confusion in the days before there was a national government, when money of one state was worthless in the next and when America lacked solid credit at home and abroad because debts were evaded. The keeping of contracts and the payment of debts had been part of his basic philosophy of sound government since his early days in the Virginia legislature. He believed it was vital for the nation's future to insist that all financial promises be firmly honored, and that in the long run that was the only real relief for America's people, no matter what immediate hardships it might cause.

His opinion in the case of *Sturges vs. Crowninshield* was one that reflected the condition of the times, his own conservative viewpoint, and his belief that the Constitution would be sapped by conceding any power of financial regulation to the states. In itself it had little lasting effect, but his boldness in asserting his views historically built one more step in extending the powers of national government and the supremacy of the Court.

The case of *Sturges vs. Crowninshield* was a test of a bankruptcy law passed by New York State for the relief of insolvent debtors. A New Yorker, Richard Crowninshield, borrowed about $1,500 from Josiah Sturges of Massachusetts and signed two notes promising to pay it back. Twelve days after Crowninshield signed the notes, New York passed its law to wipe out the debts of those who could show that they had no money.

When Sturges tried to collect his debt, Crowninshield claimed protection under the new state law. Sturges sued him in the Federal Circuit Court of Massachusetts. The judges were divided on whether New York had a right to pass such a law and whether it violated the contract clause of the Constitution, and the case was certified to the Supreme Court.

Marshall ruled, with the majority of the Court agreeing, that any state law which attempted to cancel debts made before that law was passed violated the Constitution. He held that a state could not reach into the past to wipe out liability for a debt. The New York law, he pointed out, "liberates the person of the debtor and discharges him from all liability for any debt previously contracted" and that was directly against the Constitution.

"In the case at the bar," Marshall said, "the defendant has given his promissory note to pay the plaintiff a sum of money on or before a certain day. The contract binds him to pay that sum on that day; and this is its obligation. Any law which releases . . . this obligation must, in the literal sense of the word, impair it." He said the contract clause of the Constitution clearly was meant to include such contracts as "between man and man for the payment of money." A contract was a moral pledge, a private agreement, he held, and no state had a right to interfere with the carrying out of its terms.

But then Marshall went beyond the immediate case before the Court to suggest that the Constitution also protected contracts from being broken even if those contracts were signed after a state had passed a bankruptcy law. He argued that no state had a right to promise a borrower that if he got into financial difficulties in the future he could take advantage of a bankruptcy law to wipe out his debt. What that part of his decision really amounted to was a declaration that states could not enact bankruptcy and insolvency laws, except in a very limited way. A law might be passed to keep an insolvent borrower out of debtor's prison, but not to cancel his debt entirely if at some future time he was able to get back on his feet and was then in a financial position to pay.

There was an immediate and growing storm of protest. The Court was blamed for trying to keep the states from coming to the aid of the people in the midst of a depression. Criticism was bitter and unrelenting, and even Marshall's fellow Justices finally decided he had gone too far. They repudiated that part of his decision in a later case in which the Court majority went against him and held that states could pass bankruptcy laws to ease the troubles of insolvent debtors.

In that later case of *Ogden vs. Saunders,* Marshall was the lone dissenter. It was the only time he wrote a dissent from the Court opinion on a question of constitutional law. He held out to the end, as a minority of one, against all state laws that interfered with obligations of contracts. The law that survived permitted states to apply "reservation clauses" to future private contracts between citizens of the same state, as long as their bankruptcy laws did not affect citizens of other states.

Marshall's third opinion in 1819, in the case of *McCulloch vs. Maryland,* vitalized the Constitution. There were some who would say that he even rewrote the Constitution. Great Justices of the Supreme Court who followed him to the bench more than a century afterwards agreed that the United States might never have become the nation it was except for Marshall's concept of national powers in what probably was the most far-reaching of his opinions.

With it, he helped make the Constitution a living thing,

capable of growth and of keeping pace with the advancement of the American people. Through it, he extended to Congress just about all the law-making power it would ever require to meet the nation's changing needs. By it, he affirmed as in no other way the supremacy of national government.

It was a wordy and repetitious opinion that borrowed heavily from much that already had been written about the Constitution and also from the lawyers who argued the case, and it wandered off into discussions important only to people of those times, but it was the heart of Marshall's constitutional doctrine. It was an opinion that also was thoroughly hated, as he was, by the advocates of states' rights, by the supporters of slavery, and by thousands of people who considered the decision a bulwark of conservative power and wealth.

The case directly before the Court was an outgrowth of the troubles of the Bank of the United States, which had its charter under attack in Congress and was being threatened with destruction by tax laws passed in half a dozen states. Maryland had been one of the first states that tried to tax the national bank out of business. The bank set up a branch in Baltimore and refused to pay the state tax or print its banknotes on stamped paper it was required to buy from the state, and Maryland brought suit against the cashier, William McCulloch.

It came before the Supreme Court on the question of whether the Maryland tax law was constitutional, but the much larger issue was whether a state could regulate an agency of the national government and whether Congress had power in the first place to establish the Bank of the United States. Daniel Webster, William Pinkney and Attorney General William Wirt as attorneys for the bank, opposed by Luther Martin, Joseph Hopkinson and Walter Jones for the state of Maryland, argued the questions for nine days.

Even in Washington, where eloquent speech-making was

no novelty, the Court's oratorical show drew such crowds of fashionable ladies and gentlemen that Justice Story reported "the hall was full almost to suffocation and many went away for want of room." But with the verbal fireworks over, there were only a few spectators in Court, mostly lawyers there on business, when Marshall read his historic opinion on March 6, 1819. His opening words made it clear that more than the Bank of the United States was involved, as heated an issue as that then was.

"A sovereign state denies the obligation of a law of the Union," he said. "The Constitution of our country, in its most vital parts, is to be considered; the conflicting powers of the government of the Union and of its members," and an opinion is to be given "which may essentially influence the great operations of government."

Since the states as well as the nation had certain powers, "the supremacy of their respective laws, when they are in opposition, must be settled," he went on. But the national government "is the government of all; its powers are delegated by all; it represents all and acts for all" and therefore the states must be bound by national laws. This was not a question which had been left to "mere reason," Marshall said, "because the people have, in express terms, decided it, by saying *this Constitution and the laws of the United States which shall be made in pursuance thereof . . . shall be the supreme law of the land.*"

The Constitution enumerated some of the powers granted to the national government and implied others, because it would be impossible to list them all, he said. "A constitution to contain an accurate detail of all the subdivisions of which its great powers will admit, and of all the means by which they may be carried into execution . . . could scarcely be embraced by the human mind. Its nature therefore requires that only its great outlines should be marked. . . . In considering this question then, we must never forget, that it is a *constitu-tion* we are expounding."

While the power of Congress to establish a bank was not among those listed in the Constitution, Marshall said it flowed from "the great powers to lay and collect taxes, to borrow money, to regulate commerce" and that a government "entrusted with such ample powers, on the due execution of which the happiness and prosperity of the nation so vitally depends, must also be trusted with ample means for their execution."

Therefore, to the enumeration of specific powers, the Constitution also added the implied powers stated in the direct words of the Constitution itself, giving Congress the right to make *all laws which shall be necessary and proper for carrying into execution the foregoing powers, and all other powers vested by this Constitution in the government of the United States, or in any department or officer thereof.*

"This provision is made in a Constitution intended to endure for ages to come," Marshall said, "and consequently to be adapted to the various crises of human affairs. To have prescribed the means by which government should, in all future time, execute its powers . . . would have been an unwise attempt to provide, by immutable rules, for the exigencies which . . . can best be provided for as they occur." He then came to a sweeping extension of power to Congress: "Let the end be legitimate, let it be within the scope of the Constitution, and all means which are appropriate to that end, which are not prohibited, but consist with the letter and spirit of the Constitution, are constitutional."

In revealing once and for all the expansive scope of the powers conferred by the Constitution upon the national government, he interpreted it to give Congress all the authority it would ever need to meet as yet unforeseeable "crises of human affairs." This became the famed doctrine of "implied powers," resting on the "necessary and proper" clause of the

Constitution. Marshall repudiated Jefferson's idea of strictly confining those powers only to what was "absolutely necessary" as a concept that would hamstring the government. He gave Congress its will to carry out the enumerated powers of the Constitution by whatever means were "plainly adapted" or "appropriate."

Turning to the immediate case before the Court, concerning the Bank of the United States, he declared that "it is the unanimous and decided opinion of this Court that the act to incorporate the Bank of the United States is a law made in pursuance of the Constitution, and is part of the supreme law of the land," and that the bank had a right to establish a branch in Maryland. That having been decided, the question was, "Whether the State of Maryland may, without violating the Constitution, tax that branch?" His answer was, in effect, that a properly empowered law of the national Congress was the supreme law in any conflict with laws of the states.

America's system of government, Marshall said, was based on "a principle which so entirely pervades the Constitution . . . is so interwoven with its web, so blended with its texture, as to be incapable of being separated from it without rending it to shreds." He said: "This great principle is that the Constitution and the laws made in pursuance thereof are supreme; that they control the constitution and laws of the respective states, and cannot be controlled by them."

Congress was given the power to create the bank, he held, but Maryland had assumed a power to tax it that "involves the power to destroy" and there was "a plain repugnance in conferring on one government a power to control the constitutional measures of another." He went on: "If we apply the principle for which the State of Maryland contends to the Constitution generally, we shall find it capable of changing totally the character of that instrument. We shall find it capable of arresting all the measures of government, and of prostrating it at the foot of the states. . . . If the states may tax one instrument employed by the government in the execution of its powers, they may tax any and every other instrument."

States might try to tax the mail, the mint, patent rights, customs papers, he said, and might tax everything the government did and "defeat all the ends of government." But, "This was not intended by the American people. They did not design to make their government dependent on the states. . . . The question is, in truth, a question of supremacy; and if the right of the states to tax the means employed by the general government be conceded . . . the supreme law of the land is empty and unmeaning."

The Court, he ruled, was convinced "that the states have no power, by taxation or otherwise, to retard, impede, burden, or in any manner control the operations of constitutional laws enacted by Congress to carry into execution the powers vested in the general government. . . . We are unanimously of the opinion that the law passed by the legislature of Maryland imposing a tax on the Bank of the United States is unconstitutional and void."

Having, in one great sweep, forever expanded the powers of Congress and national government, placed the Federal government in supremacy over the individual states when their laws were in conflict, and having told the states they could enforce no legislation to hamper the carrying out of Federal legislative policies, Marshall ended his busy six weeks of 1819. With the Court term over, he hurried out of Washington and back home to Richmond and to Polly. But behind him a thunder of protest shook the land.

18

JOHN MARSHALL's interpretation of the Constitution became the center of a storm that swirled up around him and the Supreme Court. It grew out of many passions and discontents and spread from the people to the state legislatures and finally to Congress, where in nearly every session for the rest of Marshall's life attempts were made to limit or weaken the Court and his influence upon it.

He and the Court were hated for upholding the Bank of the United States, which many blamed for their depression hardships. There were those who accused the Court of keeping the states from passing debtors' relief laws, others whose enmity came from the desire for free and easy credit and freedom from national controls that limited charters, contracts and speculation. The Court was charged with making rulings that fostered monopolies, corporations and financial trusts, and with interfering with free trade.

Another storm burst upon the Court from the black clouds of slavery. With passions aroused over the Missouri Compromise some Southern plantation owners feared the Supreme Court had given Congress authority to interfere with slavery. Marshall's name became a swear word in parts of the South and his opinions were cited with outrage and with demands that the Court be stopped before it could do more to interfere with "state sovereignty."

In the North as well as the South there was a growing democracy that demanded more direct voice for the people through local government and less centralized national power, and the Court had made itself a symbol of nationalism. Marshall would make no apology for that; his faith was in a strong Union and he was determined to strengthen it more. But for mixed and differing reasons, many groups had found him a common target for their woes and began to raise the cry that the Supreme Court was "robbing the people of their right to govern themselves."

Marshall had hardly delivered his opinion in *McCulloch vs. Maryland* before what was then probably the nation's most influential newspaper, Hezekiah Niles's *Weekly Register*, launched a series of attacks that were picked up by other newspapers across the country. In articles that ran for weeks, Niles detailed his reasons for charging: "A deadly blow has been struck at the sovereignty of the states, and from a quarter so far removed from the people as to be hardly accessible to public opinion."

In New York, the *General Advertiser* called the decision one that was "in defiance of human rights, human joys and divine commandments" and said of Marshall and the other justices that "their reason and their judgment has forsaken them." As the press battle raged, Virginia's Republican political machine took up the protest. Marshall's old enemy, Spencer Roane, head of the Virginia high court and the man Jefferson once had hoped to make Chief Justice in Marshall's place, wrote a series of articles in Virginia papers analyzing and attacking *McCulloch vs. Maryland*. They were signed with a pen name but everyone knew who wrote them. Marshall, finally stung by some of the criticism he considered unfair, departed from his rule of silence long enough to write an equally anonymous answer in the form of two essays published in a Philadelphia newspaper.

He soon found a stronger answer. A case appeared on the Court's docket that presented a direct challenge to its right to review state court decisions involving Federal authority. Marshall made it another platform for his constitutional doctrines and rejected an attempt to silence the Court. He affirmed not only the right of Federal courts to weigh the rulings of state courts but the duty of the national judiciary to protect the government and the Constitution from attacks by the states. Against growing disunity, threats of secession, defiance of Federal law and talk of nullification, and against those who demanded the right of each "sovereign state" to decide for itself what national laws to obey, Marshall set still stronger precedent that the Supreme Court was final and supreme.

In itself, as in so many of the cases upon which his most important opinions rested, the case of *Cohens vs. Virginia* was a minor one, except that the State of Virginia was the defendant, protesting against having its "sovereign" authority questioned by the Federal government. The case grew out of a petty crime, no more serious than the sale of a few lottery tickets.

Congress had authorized the Federal city of Washington to organize a National Lottery and to sell tickets that would give lucky winners some $10,000 in prizes. The funds raised were to be used for public buildings and other civic improvements. Two brothers who were peddling chances in the lottery, P. J. and M. J. Cohen, went over into Virginia, where they were promptly arrested for selling some tickets to William Jennings of Norfolk. It was against the law in Virginia to sell chances in any lottery not authorized by the state and the Cohen brothers were found guilty by a Norfolk court and fined one hundred dollars.

Some of the highest paid lawyers in America soon appeared to represent the Cohens and to make a test suit. They carried

the case from the state court to the Supreme Court on a writ
of error, claiming a conflict between a state law and an act
of Congress. When *Cohens vs. Virginia* reached the Supreme
Court in 1821, Virginia insisted the Court had no right even
to hear the case. The Court had no authority to call a "sovereign state" before it, Virginia's attorneys said, and no jurisdiction to consider an appeal from a state court or to review
the judgment of that court.

Virginia contended that each state could interpret the Constitution for itself, even if every state interpreted it differently.
Its lawyers admitted that might cause confusion among the
states, but said that was an "irremedial mischief" built into
the constitutional system. If states were to remain free of
Federal domination, Virginia argued, state judges could not
have their decisions questioned by the Supreme Court.

Senator James Barbour of Virginia, acting as counsel for
his state, moved to have the Cohens' case dismissed. He went
further and suggested that if the Court tried to assume jurisdiction it might result in "exciting the hostility of the state
governments" to the point of endangering the nation, because
some states were already questioning "how long this government shall endure."

As attorney for the Cohens, William Pinkney argued that
the Supreme Court must have final and absolute decision and
that to deny it appellate jurisdiction over cases involving the
Constitution or national law that arose in the state courts
would mean "every other branch of Federal authority might
as well be surrendered." For the Supreme Court to silence
itself in such cases, he said, would mean turning the Union
back to the days when it had been "a mere league or con-
federacy." David Ogden, also acting for the Cohens, denied
that "there is any such thing as a sovereign state, independent
of the Union."

Marshall's opinion was the boldest he had delivered in his
twenty years as Chief Justice and in the face of the attacks

against the Court, perhaps was also his bravest. It was a ringing declaration of national power, of Union, and of the principles of the Constitution which the Court intended to defend. He established the jurisdiction of the Court with arguments that would be cited down the years whenever its supremacy was questioned.

"The American states, as well as the American people, have believed a close and firm union to be essential to their liberty and to their happiness," he said. "They have been taught by experience that this union cannot exist without a government for the whole; and they have been taught by the same experience that this government would be a mere shadow, that must disappoint all their hopes, unless invested with large portions of that sovereignty which belongs to independent states."

He quoted the words of the Constitution that *the judges in every state shall be bound thereby, anything in the constitution or laws of any state to the contrary notwithstanding.* The national government, though limited in its objects, "is supreme with respect to those objects," he said. "With the ample powers confided to this supreme government . . . are connected many express and important limitations on the sovereignty of the states . . . but in addition to these, the sovereignty of the states is surrendered in many instances where surrender can only operate to the benefit of the people, and where, perhaps, no other power is conferred on Congress than a conservative power to maintain the principles established in the Constitution. The maintenance of these principles in their purity is certainly among the great duties of the government."

One of the instruments chosen to maintain the principles of the Constitution was the Judicial department. "It is authorized to decide all cases, of every description, arising under the Constitution or laws of the United States," Marshall said. "From this general grant of jurisdiction no exception is made of those cases in which a state may be a party. . . . One of the express objects for which the Judicial department was established, is the decision of controversies between states, and between a state and individuals."

Virginia's contention that each state had the sovereign right to interpret the Constitution for itself, he said, would "prostrate" the government and its laws. "What power of government could be executed by its own means, in any state disposed to resist its execution by a course of legislation? The laws must be executed by individuals acting within the several states. If these individuals may be exposed to penalties, and if the Courts of the Union cannot correct the judgments by which these penalties may be enforced, the course of government may be, at any time, arrested by the will of one of its members. Each member will possess a *veto* on the will of the whole."

The Constitution was "framed for ages to come, and is designed to approach immortality as nearly as human institutions can approach it," he said. "Its course cannot always be tranquil. It is exposed to storms and tempests, and its framers must be unwise statesmen indeed, if they have not provided it, so far as nature will permit, with the means of self-preservation from the perils it may be destined to encounter. No government ought to be so defective in its organization as not to contain within itself the means of securing the execution of its own laws.... Courts of justice are the means most usually employed; and it is reasonable to expect that a government should repose on its own courts rather than on others. There is certainly nothing in ... our Constitution ... which would justify the opinion that the confidence reposed in the states was so implicit as to leave in them and their tribunals the power of resisting or defeating, in the form of law, the legitimate measures of the Union."

He summed up the first point of jurisdiction by announcing that the Court could "perceive no reason ... for introducing an exception which the Constitution has not made; and we think that the judicial power, as originally given, extends to all cases arising under the Constitution or a law of the United States, whoever may be the parties."

But Virginia had argued that under the Constitution's Eleventh Amendment the appellate power of the Court could not be exercised over the judgment of a state court. That argument, Marshall said, was based mainly on the idea that the Federal courts were as foreign to those of a state as the courts of some foreign nation might be, but it was an argument "not founded on any words in the Constitution" because the national government also was the government of the states.

"In war we are one people. In making peace we are one people. In all commercial regulations we are one and the same people," he said. "In many other respects the American people are one, and the government which is alone capable of controlling and managing their interests in all these respects, is the government of the Union. It is their government, and in that character they have no other. . . . The people have declared that in the exercise of all the powers given for these objects it is supreme. It can, then, in effecting these objects, legitimately control all individuals or governments within the American territory."

Since the Supreme Court had power to decide whether the constitution or law of a state was acceptable or "absolutely void" in relation to the Constitution and laws of the United States, he asked, "Is it unreasonable that it should also be empowered to decide on the judgment of a state tribunal enforcing such unconstitutional law? Is it so very unreasonable as to furnish a justification for controlling the words of the Constitution?"

He answered for the Court: "We think not. We think that, in a government acknowledgedly supreme with respect to objects of vital interest to the nation, there is nothing inconsistent . . . in making all its departments supreme. . . . The exercise of the appellate power over those judgments of the state tribunals which may contravene the Constitution or laws of the United States is, we believe, essential to the attainment of those objects."

Therefore the Constitution gave to the Supreme Court "appellate jurisdiction in all cases arising under the Constitution, laws, and treaties of the United States." The words of the Constitution were "broad enough to comprehend all cases of this description in whatever court they may be decided." And the Court was "unanimously of the opinion that the objections to its jurisdiction are not sustained" and that Virginia's motion to dismiss the case should be overruled. Said Marshall, "Motion denied."

But, having claimed the jurisdiction of the Court in *all* cases under the Constitution or *any* law of the United States in *any* court where there might be a conflict of Federal and state law, even to the point of bringing a "sovereign state" itself before the Court as a defendant, Marshall characteristically allowed Virginia a Pyrrhic victory.

With the important questions out of the way, the Court finally turned to the case of the two peddlers of lottery tickets, and Marshall held that it really involved no conflict between an act of Congress and a state law after all. By careful reading of the statute, he found that when the National Lottery was authorized its operations were restricted to the city of Washington, and therefore the brothers Cohen had no right to go peddling chances in Virginia.

On the merits of the case, the Norfolk court had been correct in convicting the Cohens. So, after having taken a giant step forward, Marshall prudently took a little step back. He gave it as the opinion of the unsilenced Supreme Court that in this particular case, since no law of Congress had been violated by the state, Virginia could be allowed to exercise its "sovereignty," and he upheld the decision against the Cohens by the Virginia court.

THE HOWL of rage over Marshall's jurisdictional decision in *Cohens vs. Virginia* echoed up and down the country. From Virginia to Kentucky and from the Carolinas north to Pennsylvania and Ohio, judges, lawyers and other respected men, along with a number of political hacks, filled the newspapers and produced full-length books to denounce Marshall and the Court. Virginia's Republicans led the attack, headed by Judge Roane, who was publicly seconded by an aging Thomas Jefferson.

Roane took up his pen to write another series of anonymous articles, some of them brilliant in their legal argument, charging that Marshall's opinion would have a "fatal effect" upon the liberties of the people. He said the Marshall Court belonged to a past generation and that Marshall exercised such influence on the other Justices that they were guilty of "culpable apathy." Jefferson wrote that it was a "very dangerous doctrine" for courts to become "ultimate arbiters" of all constitutional questions and asserted that "the Constitution has erected no such single tribunal."

Virginia's legislature, followed by legislatures in Kentucky and South Carolina, rose in full revolt against the Court with resolutions of defiance of Federal law and its rulings, and demands for Congressional "protection" against invasion of states' rights. Ohio openly refused to obey Federal bank laws and half a dozen other states, with less forceful action, rejected various government controls.

In Washington, Congress became the battleground of efforts that were to go on year after year to curtail the Supreme Court. Attempts were made to put through bills to transfer much of the Court's jurisdiction to the Senate, to pack the Court with new Justices by increasing its membership, to forbid it to declare state laws unconstitutional, or to require decisions by three-fourths of the Justices instead of a simple majority. But all the Congressional efforts that were made during Marshall's lifetime failed.

During the hearings on *Cohens vs. Virginia* Marshall had taken a few hours out to administer the oath of office for a second time to re-elected President Monroe, after the Court privately gave its opinion that it would be legal to postpone the inauguration a day because March 4 fell on a Sunday.

Marshall and the Court later gave Monroe another private opinion that might have improved Marshall's popularity if it could have been made public. A bill had been put through Congress to build roads and make rivers navigable, and Monroe questioned the use of Federal funds for such purposes. Monroe asked the Court for a private opinion on the constitutionality of the measure and the Justices advised the President that the government could legally use some of its money for such national improvements, which were being much clamored for by some of Marshall's most outspoken opponents.

Gradually some of the public furor over the Court subsided. Americans became more interested in the country's expanding economic growth and trade than in political quarrels over the structure of government, and a case came to the Court that for a change won it the enthusiastic approval of nearly everybody. For a time, Marshall and the Court became almost national heroes. It was a case that gave him an opportunity to deliver one of his greatest state papers.

Marshall's opinion in *Gibbons vs. Ogden* would be cited one hundred and forty years later as the controlling precedent when another Supreme Court sustained the Civil Rights Act of 1964. But its popularity in 1824 was not for its incidental doctrines, but for striking down a steamboat monopoly. It became famous as the "Steamboat Case." What Marshall's opinion did was no less than to guarantee the development of interstate commerce in the United States.

The hoarse whistle of the steamboat had heralded a new era in American transportation and commerce when Robert Fulton's *Clermont* made the first commercially successful voyage up the Hudson River from New York to Albany in 1807. Fulton and his partner and financial backer, Robert Livingston, envisioned a monopoly that would spread steamboats they controlled over the rivers and lakes of the entire nation, and New York State gave them a good start by granting them a thirty-year monopoly on steam navigation within the waters under its jurisdiction.

But many others began to build steamboats and operate them and rivalry grew among the states. New York and New Jersey passed laws to deny each other's steamboats the use of their ports under retaliatory threats of confiscating boats that violated their jealously guarded state waters. Connecticut barred Livingston-Fulton boats, Ohio imposed restrictions on out-of-state steamboats, and soon Louisiana, Georgia, Massachusetts and other states started granting exclusive monopolies to various operators.

The commercial warfare among the states threatened the free trade of the nation. If states could pass laws against one another to limit the passage of unauthorized steamboats through their waters, they might prohibit other commerce.

Each state might make its boundary a transportation and trade barrier to other states. Such commercial wars had led to the abandonment of the Confederation and the adoption of the Constitution, which was meant to prevent them. But nobody had ever thoroughly spelled out or really defined as a working law the Constitution's rather vague promise of free commerce among the states. Nobody was sure that steamboat navigation was even legally a part of commerce.

Two steamboat operators, Thomas Gibbons and Aaron Ogden, worked out a plan to evade the Livingston-Fulton monopoly. Ogden ferried freight and passengers to a Hudson River point where Gibbons' boats picked them up and carried them on to places in New Jersey. When Livingston and Fulton objected and threatened action, Ogden agreed to pay them a license fee to operate under their franchise, but Gibbons refused. Gibbons started running his boats in direct competition with his former partner and in defiance of the monopoly.

Ogden went into court in New York to get an injunction against Gibbons. But Gibbons, in his defense, argued that he held a coasting license from the Federal government which entitled him to bring vessels into any port he wished and to navigate any waters within the jurisdiction of the United States.

The New York courts held that was not enough to invalidate the state law and that a Federal license to sail from one port along the coast to another did not cover operating a steamboat ferry service out of New York. After various appeals and long delays the case of *Gibbons vs. Ogden* finally reached the Supreme Court. It became a test of Federal versus state law, and more important a test of the whole concept of state monopolies that restricted free interstate commerce.

Daniel Webster and William Wirt, as attorneys for Gibbons, argued the case for Federal supremacy. Against them, for Ogden and the steamboat monopoly, were New York's Attorney General Thomas Oakley and Thomas Addis Emmett, brother of a famous Irish martyr and himself a noted defender of Irish causes. They debated through five days of hearings before the Court and an impressively distinguished audience that included most of the leaders of Congress, who came down to the Capitol's basement to hear the debates.

It took the Justices several weeks to prepare a decision, not because of disagreement but because they realized they were deciding a fundamental issue upon which much of the nation's development would depend. There was added delay when Marshall slipped getting into a carriage after a White House reception and dislocated his shoulder. Kept to his room for two weeks, he wrote a long letter to Polly, tenderly recalling some of the romantic events of their courtship years before, and added, "Old men, I find, do not get over sprains and hurts as quickly as young ones." But with "plenty of time on my hands in the night as well as the day," Marshall wrote his opinion in the case of *Gibbons vs. Ogden* and finally delivered it to a crowded courtroom on March 2, 1824.

The terse wording of the commerce clause of the Constitution did not define what commerce was or specify how it should be regulated. Article One, Section 8, simply declared: "The Congress shall have power to regulate commerce with foreign nations, and among the several states, and with the Indian tribes . . . (and) to make all laws which shall be necessary and proper for carrying into execution the foregoing powers and all other powers vested by this Constitution in the Government of the United States, or in any department or officer thereof."

The New York courts had based their decision against Gibbons on a very narrow interpretation of the commerce clause, but Marshall said the Court didn't see why it should be interpreted in a limiting way. There wasn't "one sentence in the Constitution" which said it had to be narrowly defined. Since it was "an investment in power for the general advantage," it should not be interpreted so narrowly as to "deny the government those powers which the words of the grant, as generally understood, import" because to do so would "cripple the government and render it unequal" to the objects desired.

It was a common sense rule, he thought, that when in doubt over what any part of the Constitution meant its words should be taken at their face value, as they were understood by the people, without trying to read into them any narrow legal restrictions which were not intended by the plain language of those who wrote the Constitution.

"As men whose intentions require no concealment generally employ the words which most directly and aptly express the ideas they intend to convey, the enlightened patriots who framed our Constitution and the people who adopted it must be understood to have employed words in their natural sense, and to have intended what they have said," he explained. So he asked what was the "natural sense" of the words in the Constitution that *Congress shall have power to regulate commerce with foreign nations, and among the several states, and with the Indian tribes,* and he said that obviously the "subject to be regulated is commerce" and "to ascertain the extent of the power, it becomes necessary to settle the meaning of the word."

Attorneys for the monopolists "would limit it to traffic, to buying and selling, or to the interchange of commodities, and do not admit it comprehends navigation," Marshall said, but that would restrict a general term, which could be applied to many things, to just one of its meanings.

"Commerce undoubtedly is traffic, but it is something more," he said. "It is intercourse. It describes the commercial intercourse between nations, and parts of nations, in all its branches, and is regulated by prescribing rules for carrying on that intercourse. . . . All America understands, and has uniformly understood, the word commerce to comprehend navigation. It was so understood, and must have been so understood, when the Constitution was framed. The power over commerce, including navigation, was one of the primary objects for which the people of America adopted their government."

He asked, "To what commerce does this power extend?" and answered with the sweeping definition: "It has, we believe, been universally admitted that these words comprehend every species of commercial intercourse. . . . No sort of trade can be carried on . . . to which this power does not extend."

The subject to which the power was applied was commerce "among the several states." The word "among," he said, "means intermingled with. A thing which is among others is intermingled with them." Therefore, "commerce among the states cannot stop at the external boundary-line of each state, but may be introduced into the interior." That did not mean states could not regulate certain kinds of commerce within a state, such as "that which is completely internal, which is carried on between man and man in a state, or between different parts of the same state," as long as "it does not extend to or affect other states."

But in regulating commerce, Marshall went on, "the power of Congress does not stop at the jurisdictional lines of the several states. It would be a very useless power if it could not pass those lines. The commerce of the United States . . . is that of the whole United States. Every district has a right to participate in it. The deep streams which penetrate our country in every direction pass through the interior of almost every state in the Union, and furnish the means of exercising this right. If Congress has the power to regulate it, that power must be exercised whenever the subject exists. If it exists within the states . . . then the power of Congress may be exercised within a state. . . . The power of Congress, then, whatever it may be, must be exercised within the territorial jurisdiction of the several states."

So the next question to decide was, "What is this power?" Marshall answered: "It is the power to regulate; that is, to prescribe the rule by which commerce may be governed. This power, like all others vested in Congress, is complete in itself, may be exercised to its utmost extent, and acknowledges no limitations other than are prescribed in the Constitution. . . . The power of Congress, then, comprehends navigation within the limits of every state in the Union. . . . It may, of consequence, pass the jurisdiction line of New York, and act upon the very waters to which the prohibition now under consideration applies."

States, in regulating their own internal affairs, might pass laws that interfered with or were contrary to acts of Congress, "to deprive a citizen of a right," such as the steamboat monopoly law of New York. In that case, Marshall held, "the acts of New York must yield to the law of Congress."

When a state law came into conflict with an act of Congress, they were not "like equal opposing powers," he said, because "the framers of the Constitution foresaw this state of things, and provided for it by declaring the supremacy not only of itself but of the laws made in pursuance of it. . . . In every such case the act of Congress . . . is supreme; and the law of the state . . . must yield to it."

There were those who by their narrow interpretations and reasoning, would "explain away the Constitution of our country and leave it a magnificent structure . . . to look at, but totally unfit to use," he said. Such arguments "may so entangle and perplex the understanding as to obscure principles which were before thought quite plain," but in such a case, he believed, it was "peculiarly necessary to recur to safe and fundamental principles, to sustain those principles. and when sustained, to make them the tests of the arguments to be examined."

Having defined interstate commerce according to the "plain

words" of the Constitution itself, in the broadest meaning of those words, Marshall came back to the steamboat monopoly and demolished it by announcing the decision of the Court: "Decree of Court of New York reversed and annulled and bill of Aaron Ogden dismissed."

America's response was immediate and approving. Some die-hard Republicans were displeased and some guardians of "state sovereignty" were infuriated by what they considered another Court "invasion" of states' rights, but their protests were drowned in the chorus of praise for Marshall and the Court from the great majority of Americans. Newspapers generally hailed the ruling as promising a new economic unity for the nation, a great flowering of transportation, trade and business growth, and a freedom for commerce to spread through the states that no longer could make each boundary a barrier.

New York became a free port for all America. Within two years steamboat navigation of the nation's rivers and lakes more than doubled. Travel through areas formerly covered only by stagecoach was cheaper. Communication was quickened and the settlement of new lands was spread. Transportation of anthracite coal was easier and less expensive. New England's manufacturers as well as factory owners elsewhere, merchants, builders, investors and promoters, all benefited from the freeing of interstate commerce.

In the not too distant future steam railroading would be encouraged by the guidelines Marshall had set, and in years long after his time, the ruling would affect telegraph, telephone, oil and gas pipelines, and enduringly hundreds of other things, tangible and intangible, from trucks and highways to protections of civil rights, in the freedom to cross state lines. Perhaps Marshall saw that future only dimly, but he had the vision to see it, and the daring to use it for a guarantee of national progress that was in the stream of history.

→»» CHAPTER «←

20

ALL OVER the United States there were glorious celebrations of the fiftieth anniversary of the Declaration of Independence on the Fourth of July, 1826, but on that day two men of opposite views who had helped build the nation from its founding died. One was John Marshall's old friend, John Adams, who had appointed him Chief Justice, and the other his old opponent, Thomas Jefferson. An age died with them, the age of America's beginnings, to which Marshall also belonged.

For a man in his seventies Marshall was vigorous, alert, clear-minded, and determined not to give up the fight for the philosophy of government in which he believed, but the rising spirit of the new democracy filled him with alarm. There were times when he wished he were out of public life entirely and away from the turmoil in Washington. "A person as old as I am feels that his home is his place of most comfort, and his old wife the companion in the world in whose society he is most happy," he wrote Polly. "I long to leave this bustling busy scene and to return to the tranquility of my family and my farm."

But there were battles yet to be fought and work for the

Court to do. Marshall had been more than usually pleased the year before, when he administered the oath of office on March 4, 1825, to President John Quincy Adams, not only because of the pride he felt in the inauguration of his old friend's son, but because the election kept Andrew Jackson out of the White House for a time. Marshall thoroughly admired Adams, thought him a sound man of the old school of leaders who would keep the nation strong. But in the eyes of the country, if not in Marshall's, President Adams became a failure.

Adams almost entirely lacked the personality to hold the support of the public and his fortunes went down while those of Jackson rose. Marshall watched apprehensively through Adams' declining administration as America again split into new political factions and party quarrels that he deplored. He little understood the democracy of this new age that wasn't his, and saw it only as a divisive force. Still a Federalist, the last of the Federalists in a party long dead, Marshall was left with no choice but a embrace the wing of the Republican party which best voiced his philosophy.

The Republicans had broken in two, one group the conservative Jeffersonians who believed in Federal power, if somewhat limited power, in government aid to banks and business, and government spending for internal improvements; the other, the liberal Jeffersonians, including an enormously increased number of new voters who had risen against the old establishment.

Conservatives, under the leadership of Henry Clay, took the traditional name of National Republicans and offered Adams for re-election in 1828. Rallying around Jackson, the opposing liberals gloried in what had once been almost a curse-word and openly called themselves "Democrats" or "Democratic-Republicans." Jackson himself had praised the once-horrid word by saying he was for the "Democracy of Numbers," and so were they. Four years before, only about 350,000 Americans had voted for President. But in 1828, some 1,155,000 would vote, thanks to new Western states that had granted them that right, and to suffrage battles finally won in legislatures of some of the older states.

Marshall, following his long policy of keeping the Court above political controversies, had not voted in nearly a quarter of a century because there was no secret balloting and a voter had to declare his preference in public by calling out his choice for everyone to hear. His last vote had been against Jefferson in 1804. But in 1828, against Jackson, he felt he couldn't remain silent. He let it become known through the newspapers that *if* he voted, he would support Adams.

But his influence on the election was none. Jackson captured more than sixty-eight per cent of the electoral votes and Marshall retired to the seclusion of his Court and after that tended more than ever to avoid being directly involved in party politics. He soon wrote Polly that while some of his old friends, such as aging John Randolph, seemed "as much absorbed in the party politics of the day" as in times long past, "it is very different with me." He remained ever a political man, with definite views of what was good for the nation, but his battles were waged from the platform of the Court.

The Court itself was having serious problems. Justice Brockholst Livingston had died, to be replaced by former Secretary of the Navy Smith Thompson. Then Justice Thomas Todd, with the whole West to cover once a year on his circuit, had died, a victim of illnesses brought on by the hardships of his road-jolting tasks. President Adams appointed Robert Trimble of Kentucky to take his place, but although Trimble was twenty-two years younger than Marshall, he survived the rigors of his post only two years.

Marshall learned of Trimble's death at almost the same time he heard what was to him the bad news of Jackson's election as President. But Adams was still in the White House until the following March, and Marshall for the first time since he had become Chief Justice tried to intervene in the choice of an Associate Justice to replace Trimble. Marshall asked his friend Justice Story to talk to Adams and recommend John J. Crittenden, a Kentucky Senator who had been drifting toward the conservative wing of the divided Republican party, for the Court appointment.

He also wrote a letter to conservative leader Henry Clay, urging that Crittenden be named to the Court vacancy. Marshall praised Crittenden's high character, honor and knowledge of law, and said he would be glad to "welcome Crittenden as an associate" on the Court. "Were I myself to designate the successor of Mr. Trimble, I do not know the man I could prefer to him," he told Clay, explaining that because of the "delicacy of the case" he hadn't gone directly to the President with his request. "I cannot venture, unasked, to recommend an Associate Justice to the President."

Adams got the message, took Marshall's advice, and sent Crittenden's name to the Senate, but the Senate refused to confirm the appointment. Determined to hold the place on the Court open so incoming President Jackson could fill it, the Senate rebelled against letting Adams choose a justice in his last months in office. Marshall was faced with the disturbing certainty that a Jacksonian Democrat would soon sit with him on the Court. Despite all the previous shake-ups in its membership, he had kept control and usually had managed to maneuver the other Justices into following his lead, but he felt it slipping now.

He had been seriously considering resigning himself because of his age and desire to get out of Washington and because Polly's health had become very poor. Before the election, he had confided in Story that he would resign if Adams became President again and was able to name a new Chief

Justice to succeed him. But now, rather than give Jackson that opportunity, Marshall felt forced to remain in office.

The Senate, by rejecting Crittenden's nomination, had left the Court one man short for its 1829 term. Because of the jam of work that crowded the docket, Congress previously had put through a bill to extend Court sessions by opening them the second Monday in January instead of February, thus lengthening the term to about twelve weeks before the Justices had to rush off from Washington to start their circuit travels in March. Even so, the Court was able to get through only about one-fourth of the cases waiting for it.

Being one man short was a serious matter for the aging and increasingly feeble Justices. When Marshall reached Washington in January, deeply worried over having to leave Polly ill at home, he discovered his troubles had only started. Justice Duval, who at seventy-seven was three years older than Marshall and who was so deaf it was said he had not been able to hear a Court argument for years, was sick when the term opened and unable to join the others. Thompson also was on the sick list and kept at home. Justice Johnson, considered one of the youngsters of the Court at the sunny age of fifty-eight, was injured in a stagecoach accident in South Carolina and was also kept away.

When the day came for Court to open, the only ones there were Marshall, Story and Bushrod Washington, who also was ill but able to put in an appearance. The three of them couldn't handle the work alone, so a special act was put through Congress to let them call off the whole 1829 term unless the absent members turned up within twenty days. Fortunately, they all finally arrived before the waiting period was up and, either recuperating from illness or recovering from injuries, they held Court. As ill and troubled as they were, under Marshall's still vigorous direction they managed to clear the docket of some seventy cases.

"Our sick judges have at length arrived," Marshall wrote Polly, "and we are as busy as ever we will be. I do not walk as far as I formerly did but I still keep up the practice of walking in the morning." He had been to dinner at the White House with outgoing President Adams and was to dine alone again with the President later in a socially busy week. "General Jackson is expected in the city within a fortnight," he told Polly, and Jackson had reserved a room at the same boarding house where Marshall and the Justices stayed. "I shall of course wait on him. The whole world, it is said, will be here," for the inauguration, but "I wish I could leave it all and come to you."

For the eighth time since he had been Chief Justice, Marshall administered the presidential oath on the warm and springlike Wednesday that was March 4, 1829. Ex-President Adams had refused to take part in the inaugural ceremony. Marshall, because it was his official duty, had to. General Jackson was sixty-two, and Marshall twelve years older, and according to reporters they looked equally grim. There was formal politeness between them, but nothing more.

While cannon boomed a salute and a surging crowd happily followed Jackson to the White House, Marshall walked back alone the other way to his boarding house. "People have flocked to Washington from every quarter of the United States," he wrote Polly, estimating the inaugural audience at 15,000. "A great ball was given at night to celebrate the election. I, of course, did not attend it."

Two days later, President Jackson, as one of the first acts of his administration, nominated Postmaster General John McLean for the vacancy on the Supreme Court. Marshall had expected far worse. McLean was an Ohioan with some legal talent, with a distinguished career in high public office, and had been a holdover member of Presidential cabinets ever since Monroe. But Marshall was not at all pleased by the reason for McLean's appointment to the Court.

McLean had become a Jackson supporter and some important office had to be found for him, but Jackson didn't want to keep him on as Postmaster General. McLean had old-fashioned views against using that department to dispense patronage for the newly installed Democrats who were about to introduce the spoils system into national politics. So Jackson made him a Court Justice, and Marshall resented the idea that a place on his Court should be thrown to a man as a political sop. There was some coolness between them at first. It gradually thawed as McLean was drawn into the Court's fraternity and he and Marshall grew to respect each other's ability, but McLean dissented from some of Marshall's views and often was immune to his powers of persuasion.

Glad to get out of Washington that spring of 1829, Marshall enjoyed the relaxations Richmond always gave him, the formal and elaborate lawyers' dinners, and the more easy-going gatherings where he could sit in his shirtsleeves with other men to joke, swap stories and play cards. Despite his age he was still the life of the party at the Saturday barbecues and quoit-pitching contests at Buchanan's Springs, and when he tossed a ringer his pleased whoop of laughter was as loud as a boy's. At home there was the happiness of being with his children and grandchildren and with Polly.

But there was sadness, too, in seeing how weak she had become, her health so bad. There were nights when neither of them slept two hours, when her nervous seizures came and he tried helplessly to comfort her. Night noises tormented her and in July he wrote a neighbor to ask if something couldn't be done to stop the barking of his dog at night. "The distressed, I might say distracted, situation of my wife forces me very reluctantly to make a direct application to you," he wrote. "The incessant barking of your dog has scarcely left her a night of quiet since the beginning of summer. . . . Her situation is deplorable . . . she thinks she cannot live . . ."

Yet there were other times when Polly still was able to be the gracious hostess at gatherings of their friends. Late in the fall, there was a special dinner party at the Marshall home. The guests included former Presidents Madison and Monroe, now grown old as he had, but drawn to Richmond as men chosen by Virginia, as Marshall had been, for a convention to revise the state constitution which had not been changed since the Revolutionary War. The three of them were to be the central figures in what came to be known as "The Last Meeting of the Giants."

Marshall had been reluctant to serve in the convention and had first refused, but so many Virginians pleaded with him he finally gave in. "I have acted like a girl addressed by a gentleman she does not positively dislike but is unwilling to marry," he wrote his friend Story. "She is sure to yield to the advice and persuasion of her friends." So, on October 5, 1829, he joined the other distinguished delegates to the Virginia Constitutional Convention.

The Chief Justice and the two former Presidents led the delegates into the hall at the capitol and the audience stood until the three were seated. Madison called the meeting to order, nominated Monroe to be the convention's president, and Marshall seconded it and there was no dissenting vote. In the work of the convention that followed Marshall was solidly conservative. He had come a long way from his young patriot years in the Virginia legislature when he had battled for change. Now he saw no merit in what seemed to him the weakening of long-tried and tested methods of government and he used all his prestige against the Republicans and new Democrats who wanted reform.

"Whenever he spoke, which was seldom, and only for a short time, he attracted great attention," one reporter wrote.

"His appearance was Revolutionary and patriarchal. Tall in a surtout of blue, with a face of genius and an eye of fire, his mind possessed a rare faculty of condensation; he distilled an argument down to the essence."

Monroe voted most often against him and Madison with him. When the convention reached a deadlock on the question of giving greater representation in the legislature to farmers and small property owners Marshall brought about a compromise. "If we cannot meet on the line that divides us equally," he urged, "then take the hand of friendship and make an equal compromise." But he would make no compromise with reformers who wanted to give the legislature power to recall judges of the state's courts.

"The judicial department comes home in its effects to every man's fireside," Marshall said. "It passes on his property, his reputation, his life, his all. Is it not, to the last degree, important, that (a judge) should be rendered perfectly and completely independent, with nothing to influence and control him but God and his conscience?"

Monroe as well as Madison joined him in fighting that proposal and they defeated it, leaving Virginia's judges secure against threats by the legislature to remove them for decisions that displeased the state's lawmakers. Marshall stayed in the convention as long as he could, but finally had to leave Richmond in January to hurry north for the 1830 term of the Supreme Court.

Before Court opened he received the shocking news that Justice Bushrod Washington had died. Aside from Story, Washington had been his best friend among the Justices. President Jackson lost no time appointing a successor. He nominated, and the Senate promptly confirmed, Henry Baldwin, a former Congressman from Pennsylvania who had turned from the manufacture of iron to the practice of law, and from a Federalist to a Republican to a Democrat. That again upset the balance of the Court and Baldwin as well as some of the other Justices soon began to write vigorous dissenting opinions, but Marshall usually still carried the majority.

President Jackson's strong stand for Union in the Nullification crisis, when South Carolina raised the threat of Southern states to nullify Federal law in the refusal of cotton planters to pay oppressive tariffs, won Marshall's full approval. For a time, he thoroughly admired Jackson for that, but still didn't trust the President's Democratic philosophy, and knew that as far as he and the Court were concerned Jackson considered them conservative roadblocks that stood in his way.

21

J OHN MARSHALL was not a happy man. He talked again to friends about retiring. But former President John Quincy Adams, among others, was worried over what would happen to the Court if Marshall stepped down while Jackson was President, and noted that undoubtedly some "shallow-pated wildcat . . . fit for nothing but to tear the Union to rags and tatters" would be appointed in his place. Marshall confided in Story about his "real uncertainty respecting the future" and his friend protested against his even considering the thought of retiring.

Newspapers picked up the rumor and the conservative press editorialized with alarm over such a prospect. The *New York Daily Advertiser* said Marshall's resignation as Chief Justice would be "one of the greatest calamities that could at this time befall the United States." Describing him as "the most important public character of which the Union can now boast," its editors said "the welfare of the country may depend upon the continuance of his judicial life for some time to come" and that the appointment of a successor by Jackson might be "fatal to the safety of the Union."

Marshall, of course, had no public comment to make, but

he apparently made up his mind to hang on at least until the next election, in the hope that Jackson then would be defeated. "You know how much importance I attach to the character of the person who is to succeed me," he wrote Story, "and calculate the influence which probabilities on that subject would have on my continuance in office."

The Court's grinding work in the winter of 1831 kept Marshall "too busy to be unhappy." He wrote Polly: "I rise early, pore over law cases, go to Court and return at the same hour, and pass the evening in consultation with the judges. Visitors sometimes drop in upon us, but their visits are short and we always return them by a card. . . . This winter is just like the last and the last was like a dozen of its predecessors."

But this winter there was one case on the overcrowded docket that particularly troubled him, because it brought his feelings into conflict with the letter of the law. It also made him realize how powerless the Court was to enforce the law when neither of the other two branches of government was disposed to furnish that force.

The case of *Cherokee Nation vs. Georgia* brought into Court moccasin-footed and fringe-jacketed Indians who, far from being "savages," were representatives of a highly civilized government of their own. What they pleaded for was protection that had been denied them by the Congress and by the President. The existence of the Cherokees as a people was threatened by the irate refusal of one of the states to tolerate their right to self-determination, and by white men's greed for land and for gold.

When Georgia in 1802 ceded its vast western Yazoo territory to the Federal government, it was in exchange for a large payment of money and a pledge that the Indians would be moved out of the lands as soon as that could be peaceably arranged. But the promise also was given to the Indians, under long-established treaties with the government, that until they consented to move to other lands provided for them their rights would be defended against invasion, disturbance, seizure or entry. The Creeks yielded their lands in 1825. But the Cherokees, who occupied some four million acres under many treaty agreements, refused.

The Georgia Cherokees in 1827 adopted a constitution, set up a government modeled on that of the United States, and declared themselves a sovereign independent nation. Georgia, in a fierce display of "state sovereignty" swept angry resolutions through its legislature, claiming ownership of all Cherokee territory, extending the laws of Georgia over the Indians, and annulling all laws, usages and customs of the Cherokees. Proclaiming its determination to "coerce obedience from all descriptions of people, be they white, red or black," Georgia took over the lands, broke them up into counties, and began to enforce its rule upon the Cherokee "nation."

President Jackson refused to aid the Cherokees when they appealed to him for help and instead upheld the State of Georgia. As a man whose first fame had come from fighting Indians, he had little love for any red man and his attitude was shared by most frontiersmen and Westerners as well as by Americans who had grown up on the history of Indian attacks against white settlers in new lands. Jackson also favored states' rights and, from a practical point of view, had no desire to turn the armed forces of the United States against the state of Georgia, where resistance to other Federal controls already was strong.

Meanwhile exaggerated tales of rich gold discoveries swept the Cherokee country and gold fever brought white adventurers swarming into the Indian lands. Others saw far greater wealth in the land for expanding cotton plantations. As Georgia began to enforce its proclaimed rule over the Cherokee territory, there were heated debates in Congress and many Northerners sympathized with the Indians.

The government tried to persuade the Cherokees to give up their homes, farms and enterprises in Georgia for uncultivated lands in the far western territory of what later became Oklahoma. The Cherokees sent a delegation to inspect the area and refused to accept, but whether the Indians liked it or not, Congress passed a bill to remove them to the wilderness. Again they appealed to Jackson and he told them Georgia had absolute authority over them.

Having been refused protection by the President and the Congress, the Cherokees turned to the last remaining branch of government, the Supreme Court. Former Attorney General William Wirt and others who sympathized with the Indians privately sounded out Marshall. He could give them no opinion on the legal questions involved, but wrote a cautiously-worded note that revealed his sympathy.

"I have followed the debate in both houses of Congress with profound attention and with deep interest," Marshall wrote, "and have wished, most sincerely, that both the executive and legislative departments had thought differently on the subject. Humanity must bewail the course which is pursued, whatever may be the decision of policy."

The lawyers prepared what they thought was a good case for the Cherokees and applied to the Supreme Court for an injunction to prevent Georgia from carrying out its laws against them. But before it could be heard, Georgia showed its open contempt for both the Federal courts and the Cherokee courts that it had ordered abolished by arresting an Indian, George "Corn" Tassels, for killing another man, and by bringing him before a Georgia county court for trial. He was convicted of murder and sentenced to die.

His attorneys applied to Marshall and he granted them a writ of *habeas corpus* and a stay of execution until the case could be argued in the Supreme Court. The Georgia legislature furiously rejected any "interference by the Chief Justice of the United States in the administration of the criminal laws of this state" and authorized the Governor to use "all the means at his command" to resist it. Five days later, in deliberate defiance of Marshall and the Supreme Court, George Tassels was hanged.

President Jackson turned his back on the affair. Humiliated, publicly insulted, helpless to enforce the authority of his Court, Marshall was made to realize that the Court had no power of its own to make Georgia do anything it did not wish to do. That was direct nullification by a state of Federal supremacy, but the other branches of government would do nothing, the Jackson administration had abandoned the Court, and the Court could do nothing practical to help the Cherokees.

Georgia, rejecting the right of the Court even to consider the case of *Cherokee Nation vs. Georgia,* refused to send attorneys to represent it when arguments finally were made in March, 1831. Whatever the Court decided, Georgia announced, it would ignore. Former Attorney General Wirt and attorney John Sergeant of Philadelphia represented the Cherokees. They spent two days presenting their plea for an injunction, based mainly on the claim that the Indians were a "foreign nation" whose affairs were regulated by treaty with the United States and that therefore no state had jurisdiction over them. They contended no state could take away Indian land since all land originally belonged to the Indians and could be acquired only by treaty.

Marshall, clearly distressed, made his own feelings plain from the first words of the opinion he read: "This bill is brought by the Cherokee Nation, praying an injunction to restrain the state of Georgia from the execution of certain laws of that state which, as is alleged, go directly to annihilate the Cherokee as a political society, and to seize for the use of Georgia the lands of the nation which have been assured to them by the United States, in solemn treaties repeatedly made and still in force."

If courts "were permitted to indulge their sympathies," he said, "a case better calculated to excite them can scarcely be imagined. A people, once numerous, powerful and truly independent, found by our ancestors in the quiet and uncontrolled possession of an ample domain, gradually sinking beneath our superior policy, our arts and our arms, have yielded their lands by successive treaties, each of which contains a solemn guarantee of the residue, until they retain no more of their formerly extensive territory than is deemed necessary to their comfortable subsistence. To preserve this remnant, their present application is made."

But against his sympathy for the Indians, there was the law, and he was allowed no personal feelings in interpreting that. He could allow no emotional pleas or public demands or excitements to influence him. "Before we can look into the merits of this case, a preliminary inquiry presents itself," he said. "Has this Court jurisdiction?"

The Cherokees had presented themselves before the Court as a foreign nation because that seemed the only way open to them. Under the Constitution the Court had jurisdiction in controversies between a state and the citizens of a foreign nation.

"But the relation of the Indians to the United States is marked by peculiar and cardinal distinctions," Marshall said. Indian territory was part of the United States; Indians acknowledged in their treaties that they were under the protection of the United States; Indians were subject to the control of the United States in trade and commercial regulations. "These considerations go far to support the opinion that the framers of our Constitution had not the Indian tribes in view when they opened the courts of the Union to controversies between a state . . . and foreign states."

Instead of being foreign nations they were more "domestic dependent nations . . . in a state of pupilage; their relation to the United States resembles that of a ward to his guardian." The Constitution made a clear distinction between Indians and foreign nations in the commerce clause and in the treaty power. Therefore, it was the majority opinion of the Court "that an Indian tribe or nation within the United States is not a foreign state, in the sense of the Constitution, and cannot maintain an action in the courts of the United States."

But having said that, Marshall went on to suggest that there might be a way for the Indians to gain Court jurisdiction, if they came to it with a case of a different kind. "The part of the bill which respects the land occupied by the Indians, and prays the aid of the Court to protect their possession, may be more doubtful," he said. "The mere question of right, might perhaps, be decided by this Court in a proper case, with proper parties."

It was almost an invitation to the Cherokees to find a way to come back to Court again and he had hinted broadly what argument might be heard. That was as far as he could go. But in the final words of the opinion, Marshall did throw blame on President Jackson and the Congress for not using the power that the Court lacked. "If it be true that wrongs have been inflicted, and that still greater are to be apprehended, this is not the tribunal which can redress the past or prevent the future." So, since he could rule no other way, he said, "The motion for an injunction is denied."

Attorneys for the Cherokees took his hint and immediately began preparing a better case. It would come before the Court the next term. For now, the Court was through, and he could go home to Richmond. But he went home a sad, weary and sick man. He didn't realize until he got there how really ill he was.

22

I N ALL his seventy-six years, John Marshall had never been really seriously ill. But by the time he got home to Richmond in the spring of 1831 he was having such stomach pains that friends urged him to see a doctor. He had little faith in doctors after all the years they had been treating Polly without much success and he was sure that whatever was wrong with him was temporary and he could shake it off. Besides, he had his circuit to travel, and no time to waste pampering himself.

Polly did make him a new wool cushion for the seat of his gig before he set off for the opening of court in Raleigh in May, and he sent her a note from there to tell her the cushion had helped ease the fatigue of his trip. But travel had aggravated his condition and there were days in court when he was in sweat-streaming pain. On his return to Richmond, he served on a committee to study harbor improvements, but found he was too ill to sit through long debates.

He admitted that his nerves, digestion and head were "uncomfortable," and finally was talked into seeing a doctor, but the medicine he took made him more uncomfortable than ever. Several other Richmond doctors examined him and were unable to diagnose his trouble. His suffering became such that he moved around only when necessary. "At length I suffered so much pain and became so alarmed," he wrote his friend Story, that he determined to go to Philadelphia, where Dr. Philip Syng Physick "made some examinations which led to the belief that I had probably stone in the bladder."

Dr. Physick, sometimes called "the father of American surgery," was a medical pioneer who had improved the teaching and techniques of the profession and had developed methods and instruments for what was then an unusual operation, but he advised Marshall that the chance of surviving it was about fifty-fifty. Without an operation there would be no relief from pain and probably no recovery, so Marshall took the chance.

He wrote Polly that "my hopes are sanguine as usual," that he had been visited by many old friends, had turned down an invitation to a Bar Association dinner in his honor, but had agreed to sit for the painting of his portrait for the Association clubrooms, and that "if I had my Richmond barber I think I should be quite contented." It was a chatty note, obviously intended to keep Polly from worrying, but on the same day he wrote a more sober letter to his sons. "The doctor inspires me," he said, "and I submit myself to him with a certainty that he will do all that can be done to restore me."

By modern standards the crude operation was a torture, which Marshall endured without anesthetics, and with a stoicism that amazed Dr. Physick's assistant, Dr. Jacob Randolph, who noted that the patient exhibited great fortitude, "scarcely uttering a murmur throughout the whole procedure which . . . was necessarily tedious." Randolph's detailed report concluded, "The result of the operation was a complete success."

Marshall soon was able to write Polly that "I have at length risen from my bed and am able to hold a pen. The most delightful use I can make of it is to tell you that I am getting well. . . . How much was I gratified at the line from your own hand. . . . God bless you, my dearest Polly . . ."

It was the last letter he would write to her. He returned to Richmond in December to find her dying. While he had been recovering in Philadelphia, she had been stricken, and doctors in Richmond this time had given up hope.

He had two weeks with her, sitting through the nights in lamplight by her bed. On Christmas Eve, she unlinked a locket from around her throat and gave it to him, telling him she wanted him to have it from her, and he fastened the chain around his own neck. With her hands in his, on Christmas Day, she died.

They had been married nearly fifty years, and in love that long, and his loss was something he was unable to speak about even to close friends. A year later, in Washington, his friend Story chanced to go into his room and "found him in tears over the memory of his wife."

But at some time in that period of mourning, Marshall wrote out his thoughts, not for others but for himself. The notes were later found among his papers, a long tribute, recalling all that Polly had given to enrich his life through the years. "I have lost her. And with her I have lost the solace of my life. Yet she remains the companion of my retired hours," he wrote. "When I am alone and unemployed, my mind unceasingly turns to her."

He had to leave Richmond almost immediately after Polly's funeral for the 1832 term of the Supreme Court in Washington. "I strengthen considerably," he soon wrote his youngest son Edward, "and am able, without fatigue, to walk to Court, a distance of two miles, and return to dinner. . . . I perceive no symptoms, and trust I never shall, of returning disease."

The attorneys for the Cherokees came back into Court with the "better case" Marshall had practically invited them to bring. This time, they represented not the Cherokee Nation, but a citizen of Vermont, Samuel Worcester, who had the legal standing in Court that Marshall previously had been forced to deny the Indians. As a missionary and appointed government agent in Georgia, Worcester had defied the state's proclaimed authority over the Cherokee land, and attorneys William Wirt and John Sergeant had built their new case of *Worcester vs. Georgia* on that.

Worcester was one of what were, in effect, the first Peace Corpsmen to work among the American Indians. Under an act of Congress, President John Quincy Adams had authorized a group of missionaries to work in the Cherokee reservation, helping the Indians carry out "civilizing" and educational programs with Federal funds. In addition to the Presidential appointment and Congressional authorization to be there, Worcester had been named United States postmaster at the Cherokee town of New Echota.

But Georgia, enforcing its claim to rule the Indian lands and making its own state laws, had ordered Worcester and others to get out because they hadn't been licensed by the state as white men allowed to reside in Cherokee territory. Worcester and others refused, on the grounds that they were agents of the Federal government and that Georgia had no jurisdiction over them.

Arrested by Georgia military guards, they were dragged off to prison, but were offered pardons if they would get out of Georgia and never come back. Most of the others accepted the terms, but Worcester stubbornly rejected the pardon and again challenged the state's authority. A Georgia Superior Court sentenced him to four years at hard labor. The appeal to the Supreme Court asked for the judgment of the Georgia court to be reversed because the Georgia law violated the supremacy of the Federal government.

President Jackson, who had advised the Georgians to do as they pleased about Worcester, angrily criticized the Supreme

Court for taking the case. Marshall, in his opinion, called the Georgia law an unconstitutional challenge to Presidential authority, with the implication that if Jackson continued to support the Georgians against the Cherokees he might be failing to exercise his proper duty as President.

As far as the narrow legal decision in the case went, Marshall could only strike down the one Georgia statute covering the right to be in Indian territory without the state's permission. But he went far beyond that to explore the entire question of Indian rights and to issue a sweeping indictment of white men who took Indian lands.

More than just the validity of a state law, he said, the case before the Court involved "the controlling power of the Constitution and laws of the United States, the rights . . . of a once numerous and powerful people, the personal liberty of a citizen." It had been said at the bar "that the acts of the Legislature of Georgia seize on the whole Cherokee country, parcel it out among the neighboring counties of the state, extend her code over the whole country, abolish its institutions and its laws and annihilate its political existence."

From the start of the American government the Congress had passed many acts for dealing with the Indians "which treat them as nations, respect their rights, and manifest a firm purpose to afford that protection which treaties stipulate," he said. "All these acts consider the several Indian nations as distinct political communities, having territorial boundaries, within which their authority is exclusive, and having a right to all the lands within those boundaries, which is not only acknowledged, but guaranteed by the United States."

Marshall pointed out that the very act of Congress under which Worcester had been sent into Cherokee country by President Adams declared as its purpose "providing against the further decline and final extinction of the Indian tribes adjoining the frontier settlements . . . and for introducing among them the habits and arts of civilization ... *with their own consent*."

"The treaties and laws of the United States contemplate the Indian territory as completely separated from that of the states and provide that all intercourse with them shall be carried on by the government of the Union," he said. The Constitution confers on Congress powers that "comprehend all that is required for the regulation of our intercourse with the Indians. They are not limited by any restrictions on their free actions." He held that "the whole intercourse between the United States and this nation (the Cherokees) is, by our Constitution and laws, vested in the government of the United States." Therefore:

"The Cherokee nation, then, is a distinct community, occupying its own territory, with boundaries accurately described, in which the laws of Georgia can have no force, and which the citizens of Georgia have no right to enter but with the assent of the Cherokees themselves or in conformity with treaties and with the acts of Congress. ... The act of the state of Georgia under which the plaintiff in error was prosecuted is consequently void, and the judgment a nullity. ... The acts of Georgia are repugnant to the Constitution, laws and treaties of the United States. They interfere forcibly with the relations established ... according to the settled principles of our Constitution."

Marshall ruled that Georgia's laws were "in direct hostility" to treaties that repeatedly "mark out the boundary that separates the Cherokee country from Georgia; guarantee to them all the land within their boundary; solemnly pledge the faith of the United States to restrain their citizens from trespassing on it; and recognize the pre-existing power of the (Cherokee) nation to govern itself." Georgia also had acted "with equal hostility" to the laws of Congress, he declared, and had violated the "authority of the President of the United States."

His opinion was a complete vindication of the Cherokees, of their right to their lands, laws and self-rule. It was a harsh indictment of Georgia and of all white men who tried to force Indians out of their homes and remaining property. It was a public call upon President Jackson to redeem the solemn pledge of the United States to protect the Indians.

But the Supreme Court could not force the President to act and Jackson would not act. "John Marshall has made his decision," Jackson reportedly said, "now let him enforce it!" That was the defiant statement a Congressman later quoted Jackson as having made, although there were some who thought the newspapers had made it up to embarrass him politically. But whether or not those were Jackson's actual words, that was his attitude. Jackson was on Georgia's side, and not inclined to give aid or comfort to Indians, nor was the Congress.

There was no machinery for enforcement. Under the enabling statutes then in effect, the Court could not present any legal demand for the President and the government to act. The Court could not even issue a writ that would force Georgia to release Worcester from prison since its power under the law applied only to prisoners in Federal custody.

Marshall's friend Story wrote: "The Court has done its duty. Let the nation do theirs." Some of Jackson's Northern enemies began calling for his impeachment. But Jackson's stand was overwhelmingly popular with those who favored westward expansion, and it won him far more votes than it cost. Enraged Georgians vowed they would never bow to the "alien Court." Having proved their point, however, they eventually did release Worcester from jail.

The Cherokees soon were forced out of their lands, driven out by Georgia law and by military force, and deported across the Mississippi to Oklahoma on the long sad march into the wilderness that Congress had provided for them in exchange for the rich land that white men wanted. In the end, Marshall had been able to do nothing to protect them, because the other two branches of government would do nothing, and because most Americans wanted nothing done. But he had written into the lasting record of history an indictment of the nation's conscience for its treatment of the Indians.

When Court adjourned in March, 1832, Marshall returned to the house in Richmond that was empty for him without Polly. His family worried over his being there alone and finally persuaded him to spend part of the year at Leeds Manor, the large house built by his son James in Fauquier County on the section of the Fairfax estate Marshall had given him. A wing was added to the house to provide a thick-walled study to keep out noise and Marshall shipped most of his books, papers and other belongings there.

Leeds Manor was filled with the active romping of five of his twenty-seven grandchildren and his other sons and their families lived not far away. In the mountains where he had grown up as a youth, he expected to spend his remaining years. But the pull of Richmond and his associations there was too strong to tear himself away. Leeds Manor gradually became a place for extended visits and he spent most of his time in his Richmond home.

The excitements of that Presidential election year helped dispel his loneliness. From Marshall's viewpoint, Jackson, despite his strong stand for Union in the Nullification crisis, seemed even more a foe of strong Federal government than his old enemy Jefferson had been. And Jackson, in his fight against the Bank of the United States, declared his own enmity against Marshall and the Court.

It had been Marshall's opinion in *McCulloch vs. Maryland* that had previously saved the bank. Now Jackson was attacking that institution bitterly and was determined to smash it. In July, he vetoed the bill to give the bank a new charter, and in his veto message, he criticized Marshall's opinion and rejected the Supreme Court's binding authority to decide "questions of constitutional power except where the acquiescence of the people and the states can be considered well settled."

Jackson declared in his veto message that "the opinion of the Judges has no more authority over Congress than the opinion of Congress has over the judges, and on that point the President is independent of both. The authority of the Supreme Court must not be permitted to control the Congress or the Executive when they are acting in their legislative capacities, but only to have such influence as the force of their reasoning may deserve."

To Marshall that sounded like the ghost of Jefferson risen in Jackson, as did other passages of the veto message in which Jackson spoke of "rights scrupulously reserved to the states." When the nation's voters swept Jackson back into office for a second term that November by a thundering mandate of more than seventy-six per cent of the electoral votes, Marshall saw only grave danger ahead for the Union. The political eruptions of a broader democracy were not for him.

Despite growing pressure by his family to convince him he finally should retire and spend his last years in relaxed comfort in the Virginia mountains, he decided he couldn't turn his Court over to a successor Jackson would appoint. He had hung on in the hope Jackson would be defeated, and now he would stay, for as long as he could. His health was good, his mind was clear, and he would remain Chief Justice.

When he arrived in Washington for the opening of the 1833 term in January, his friend Story thought he looked more vigorous than ever and "seemed to revive and enjoy anew his green old age." Marshall brought with him copies of a newly revised edition of his biography of Washington to present to each of his fellow Justices. He also was pleased that Story, in publishing his *Commentaries on the Constitution of the United*

States, had dedicated the work to him with a long tribute. "Posterity will assuredly confirm," Story wrote, "what the present age has approved . . . the entirety of a life adorned by consistent principles and filled up in the discharge of virtuous duty."

Always an important figure in Washington, Marshall was now treated with great respect when he appeared in public. When he attended the theater, as he still did frequently, audiences stood to applaud him. Visiting celebrities sought him out, important cases before the Court drew clusters of Senators and Congressmen among the spectators, and Marshall seemed to enjoy more than in younger years the dinners and social affairs at which he was guest of honor.

For the ninth time, he administered the presidential oath in March, 1833, at Jackson's second inauguration. The ceremony was in the House of Representatives and as the two old men faced each other, Jackson had to lean forward a little to hear Marshall's words, for his voice had become quite feeble. But aside from that, there were those who said that despite his seventy-eight years Marshall looked in better health than Jackson at sixty-six.

When the Court came back to Washington the following winter, Marshall was more concerned over the health of two of his associates than his own. Justice Johnson was too ill to attend and Justice Duval, aged and infirm, informed Marshall that he feared the term would be his last and that he intended to resign. Both were Republicans, but they had generally upheld Marshall's decisions. If the Court lost them and Jackson was given two vacancies to fill, Marshall would lose the majority that supported his constitutional principles. Justices Thompson, McLean and Baldwin had shown an increasing tendency to dissent, and that would leave only Story to rely upon.

Struggling along with Johnson absent at that 1834 term,

the Court was presented with a case questioning the constitutionality of a Kentucky law that authorized state banks to issue notes of credit, which Marshall felt was the same as issuing state currency in violation of the Federal government's sole authority to issue money. Another case seemed to him to present a challenge by New York to the Federal government's sole right to regulate navigation. Both were argued at length and in discussions among the Justices it became clear that Thompson, McLean and Baldwin wanted to uphold the two state laws.

In Marshall's view the two laws were unconstitutional. Story and Duval backed him in that and he was convinced Johnson would, if Johnson were there. That would give them a necessary majority, so Marshall maneuvered to put off any decision until the following term, when he hoped Johnson would be back in Court and Duval might change his mind about resigning.

He managed it by coming up with a rule of the Court, never known before, but which he announced as a long-standing practice: "The practice of this Court is not, except in cases of absolute necessity, to deliver any judgment in cases where constitutional questions are involved, unless four judges concur in opinion, thus making the decision that of a majority of the whole Court."

Therefore he directed the attorneys to re-argue the cases at the next term with "the expectation that a larger number of judges may then be present." His device put off the two decisions, and thereafter became a rule of the Supreme Court. But Marshall's delaying action availed him little. Before the next term began, Johnson died and Duval sent in his resignation.

President Jackson appointed James Wayne of Georgia to fill Johnson's place, and Wayne was known not to be devoted to Marshall's views of Federal supremacy. Duval's position was not filled immediately because the Senate rebelled against Jackson's first nomination. So the Court began its 1835 term again with one Justice short.

Marshall himself was ill when he opened the Court on January 12, 1835. It was to be his last term. Story wrote a friend that Marshall's "physical strength is manifestly on the decline" although he "still possesses his intellectual powers in very high vigor." The other Justices were shocked by the change in Marshall's appearance. Several times during the session, although he tried to hide it, he had attacks that obviously put him in great pain. He was suffering from a liver disease.

He carried on his work as usual. With the Court short a member he invoked the same rule he had pronounced the year before and put off the two constitutional decisions still another year. But he took an active part in all the cases argued and, despite his illness, delivered the opinion of the Court in the eleven most important decisions of the term.

During his years as Chief Justice, in the thirty-four terms of the Court over which he presided, 1,106 cases had required written opinions. Marshall wrote 509 of those opinions. Thirty-six of them involved major constitutional questions and eighty concerned problems of international law.

The Court closed the 1835 term with a Florida land case. Attorneys arguing the two sides of the title controversy had been wide apart in their views as to what was the real truth of the matter. Marshall, in deciding a motion to continue the case, observed:

"In the excitement produced by ardent controversy, gentlemen view the same object through such different media that minds not infrequently receive therefrom precisely opposite impressions." But a judge was obliged to take both sides into consideration and see more clearly than those whose views were blinded by one set of prejudices or the other. His last words from the Supreme Court bench were: "The Court . . . must see with its own eyes, and exercise its own judgment, guided by its own reason."

As the Justices left Washington that spring, Story wrote a friend about his concern for Marshall. "I pray God that he may long live to bless his country, but I confess I have many fears whether he can long be with us," he wrote. "His complaints are, I am sure, incurable, but I suppose that they may be alleviated, unless he should meet with some accidental . . . injury to aggravate them."

On his way home to Richmond, the stagecoach in which Marshall was traveling overturned and his spine was injured. He insisted, however, on traveling to Raleigh three weeks later to hold circuit court. By the time he returned to Virginia, he was so sick and weak that he gave in to the pleadings of his family to go to Philadelphia and seek medical help from the doctors who had once before saved his life.

His sons, Jacquelin, Edward and James, made the trip with him in late June. As they neared Philadelphia, Marshall reminisced a little about his memories of the city where independence had been proclaimed and the Constitution had been born when he was young, his marching through it as a soldier of the Revolution from Valley Forge, and being in Congress there.

They took rooms in Mrs. Crim's boarding house on Walnut Street. But this time, the Philadelphia doctors could not help him. He died on July 6, 1835, in little pain at the end, his mind clear. His last request was for nobody to remove the locket Polly had given him, still on its chain around his neck.

Bells in churches and public buildings tolled his passing, and it was in that ringing at Philadelphia's Independence Hall that the Liberty Bell cracked and was silenced. But what it stood for, as what John Marshall had stood for, would endure. His greatness was recognized in his own lifetime and increased through the years. The newspaper which had been the severest in its opposition to him, Niles's *Register,* said: "Next to Washington only did he possess the reverence and homage of the heart of the American people."

A century later another great Supreme Court Justice, Oliver Wendell Holmes, would say:

"There fell to Marshall perhaps the greatest place that was filled by a judge; but when I consider his might, his justice, and his wisdom, I do fully believe that if American law were to be represented by a single figure, sceptic and worshipper alike would agree that the figure could be only one alone, and that one John Marshall."

While memorial services were held across the country, Marshall's body was sent to Richmond where, according to his wish, it was taken first to his home and then to the New Burying Ground on Shockoe Hill, to be buried by the side of his wife. Two days before he died, leaving only the date to be filled in, he had written the simple inscription he wanted on his tomb:

JOHN MARSHALL
The son of Thomas and Mary Marshall
Was born on the 24th of
September, 1755; intermarried with
Mary Willis Ambler
the 3rd of January, 1783;
departed this life on the 6th day
of July, 1835.

Some Other Books About John Marshall

Adams, John Stokes, Ed., *An Autobiographical Sketch by John Marshall*, University of Michigan Press, Ann Arbor, 1937.

Beveridge, Albert J., *The Life of John Marshall*, 4 Vols., Houghton Mifflin Company, Boston and New York, 1916.

Corwin, Edward S., *John Marshall and the Constitution*, Yale University Press, New Haven, 1921.

Craigmyle, Lord, *John Marshall in Diplomacy and Law*, Charles Scribner's Sons, New York, 1933.

Dillon, John F., *John Marshall, Life, Character and Judicial Services*, Callaghan and Company, Chicago, 1903.

Konefsky, Samuel J., *John Marshall and Alexander Hamilton, Architects of the American Constitution*, The Macmillan Company, New York, 1964.

Kurland, Philip B., Ed., *James Bradley Thayer, Oliver Wendell Holmes and Felix Frankfurter on John Marshall*, The University of Chicago Press, Chicago, 1967.

Loth, David, *Chief Justice John Marshall and the Growth of the Republic*, W. W. Norton and Company, New York, 1949.

Mason, Frances Norton, *My Dearest Polly, Letters of Chief Justice John Marshall to His Wife*, Garrett & Massie, Inc., Richmond, 1961.

Oster, John Edward, *The Political and Economic Doctrines of John Marshall*, Burt Franklin, New York, 1967.

Roche, John P., Ed., *John Marshall, Major Opinions and Other Writings*, The Bobbs-Merrill Co., Inc., Indianapolis, 1967.

Surrency, Edwin C., Ed., *The Marshall Reader*, Oceana Publications, New York, 1955.

INDEX

K